LESSON 1

TOPIC
The Miraculous Power of Forgiveness

SCRIPTURES

1. **Psalm 103:12** — As far as the east is from the west, so far has He removed our transgressions from us.
2. **2 Samuel 11:1-5** — It happened in the spring of the year, at the time when kings go out to battle, that David sent Joab and his servants with him, and all Israel; and they destroyed the people of Ammon and besieged Rabbah. But David remained at Jerusalem. Then it happened one evening that David arose from his bed and walked on the roof of the king's house. And from the roof he saw a woman bathing, and the woman was very beautiful to behold. So David sent and inquired about the woman. And someone said, "Is this not Bathsheba, the daughter of Eliam, the wife of Uriah the Hittite?" Then David sent messengers, and took her; and she came to him, and he lay with her, for she was cleansed from her impurity; and she returned to her house. And the woman conceived; so she sent and told David, and said, "I am with child."
3. **2 Samuel 12:1-13** — Then the Lord sent Nathan to David. And he came to him, and said to him: "There were two men in one city, one rich and the other poor. The rich man had exceedingly many flocks and herds. But the poor man had nothing, except one little ewe lamb which he had bought and nourished; and it grew up together with him and with his children. It ate of his own food and drank from his own cup and lay in his bosom; and it was like a daughter to him. And a traveler came to the rich man, who refused to take from his own flock and from his own herd to prepare one for the wayfaring man who had come to him; but he took the poor man's lamb and prepared it for the man who had come to him." So David's anger was greatly aroused against the man, and he said to Nathan, "As the Lord lives, the man who has done this shall surely die! And he shall restore fourfold for the lamb, because he did this thing and because he had no pity." Then Nathan said to David, "You are the man! Thus says the Lord God of Israel: 'I anointed you king over Israel, and I delivered

you from the hand of Saul. I gave you your master's house and your master's wives into your keeping, and gave you the house of Israel and Judah. And if that had been too little, I also would have given you much more! Why have you despised the commandment of the Lord, to do evil in His sight? You have killed Uriah the Hittite with the sword; you have taken his wife to be your wife, and have killed him with the sword of the people of Ammon. Now therefore, the sword shall never depart from your house, because you have despised Me, and have taken the wife of Uriah the Hittite to be your wife.' Thus says the Lord: 'Behold, I will raise up adversity against you from your own house; and I will take your wives before your eyes and give them to your neighbor, and he shall lie with your wives in the sight of this sun. For you did it secretly, but I will do this thing before all Israel, before the sun.'" So David said to Nathan, "I have sinned against the Lord." And Nathan said to David, "The Lord also has put away your sin; you shall not die."

4. **Psalm 51:1-8** — Have mercy upon me, O God, according to Your lovingkindness; according to the multitude of Your tender mercies, blot out my transgressions. Wash me thoroughly from my iniquity, and cleanse me from my sin. For I acknowledge my transgressions, and my sin is always before me. Against You, You only, have I sinned, and done this evil in Your sight — that You may be found just when You speak, and blameless when You judge. Behold, I was brought forth in iniquity, and in sin my mother conceived me. Behold, You desire truth in the inward parts, and in the hidden part You will make me to know wisdom. Purge me with hyssop, and I shall be clean; wash me, and I shall be whiter than snow. Make me hear joy and gladness, that the bones You have broken may rejoice.

5. **2 Corinthians 5:21** — For He made Him who knew no sin to be sin for us, that we might become the righteousness of God in Him.

SYNOPSIS

The ten lessons in this study, ***Priceless! The Infinite Value of a Proverbs 31 Woman***, will focus on the following topics:

- The Miraculous Power of Forgiveness
- What Can Forgiveness Do for the Guilty?
- 'Help! I'm Not Perfect and Neither Is My Spouse!'

- 'How Can I Be Nice to a Difficult Husband?'
- 'To Do' or 'Not To Do' — That Is the Challenge
- There Is a Big Giver Inside You
- Your New Clothes — Strength and Honor
- 'Who's in Control — Me or My Mouth?'
- Help Me! My House Is a Mess — But Not for Long
- Practical Wisdom To Build Up Your House

The emphasis of this lesson:

God's powerful, life-changing forgiveness thoroughly washes away our sin. When we engage in true repentance and seek the Lord, He forgives completely so we can walk in the divine purpose He has prepared for us.

A Surprising Source of Wisdom

Proverbs 31 is a compelling look at womanhood and all it can be when we submit our life to the Lord. For many of us, these verses can be intimidating because we often feel like we fall so short of the ideal woman depicted in this chapter of scripture. The list of accomplishments of the Proverbs 31 woman can seem impossible to replicate.

Many historians say that Bathsheba is the author of Proverbs 31. This is Bathsheba — the wife of David; Bathsheba — the one with whom David committed adultery; Bathsheba — the one whose husband David murdered; Bathsheba — the one for whom David lied and deceived a nation. This is the very woman that history says penned the words of Proverbs 31.

To appreciate how powerful it is for Bathsheba to have written the description of a godly woman in Proverbs 31, we must first understand *who* she is. Her story begins in Second Samuel 11. In this chapter, we learn that the men of Israel had gone out to battle. But for this particular battle, David had decided to stay home. Second Samuel 11:1-5 says:

> **It happened in the spring of the year, at the time when kings go out to battle, that David sent Joab and his servants with him, and all Israel; and they destroyed the people of Ammon and besieged Rabbah. But David remained at Jerusalem.**

Then it happened one evening that David arose from his bed and walked on the roof of the king's house. And from the roof he saw a woman bathing, and the woman was very beautiful to behold. So David sent and inquired about the woman. And someone said, "Is this not Bathsheba, the daughter of Eliam, the wife of Uriah the Hittite?" Then David sent messengers, and took her; and she came to him, and he lay with her, for she was cleansed from her impurity; and she returned to her house. And the woman conceived; so she sent and told David, and said, "I am with child."

So while Bathsheba's husband, Uriah the Hittite, was fighting for his nation and serving David by fighting the people of Ammon, David was committing adultery with Bathsheba. But Bathsheba became pregnant, and this created a serious problem for both David and Bathsheba.

In an attempt to cover the sin, David called Uriah off the battlefield (*see* 2 Samuel 11:6-13). When Uriah arrived, David asked him how the battle was going and then told him, in essence, "I want you to be refreshed. Go spend some time at home with your wife, and then you can go back to the battlefield." But Uriah's integrity wouldn't allow him to do that. Uriah responded, "I can't rest and relax and lay with my wife when all the men of Israel are out on the battlefield giving their lives! I can't do that" (*see* v. 11).

But David was determined to cover his sin. He even went so far as to get Uriah drunk, hoping Uriah would head home and sleep with his wife, Bathsheba. However, Uriah still would not go home or lay with his wife because he honored God *and* the army of Israel to which he belonged.

Sin Leads to More Sin

Sin has a way of leading someone further into sin. It's like a powerful river; when you step into a flowing river, its current grabs hold of you and takes control of you. David found himself in such a river by first committing adultery and then lying about it and deceiving others to cover his tracks. It was like a river that was pulling him deeper into sin. It didn't take long before David was planning the murder of Uriah — the man who could uncover David's sin.

David wrote a letter and gave it to Uriah to give to the army's commander. In the letter, he gave instructions to send Uriah to the forefront of the battle, knowing he would be killed there. Dutifully, Uriah delivered the letter to the army's commander, unaware he was carrying his own death sentence in his hand. The commander read the king's instructions and obeyed them. Uriah was sent to the forefront of the fiercest battle while many of his fellow soldiers retreated. As predicted, Uriah died.

Believing their sin had been covered up, David married Bathsheba, but David's sin was not covered up at all.

'You Are the Man'

A prophet named Nathan visited David with a message from the Lord that revealed how *God* felt about David's sin. Second Samuel 12:1-4 says:

> Then the Lord sent Nathan to David. And he came to him, and said to him: "There were two men in one city, one rich and the other poor. The rich man had exceedingly many flocks and herds. But the poor man had nothing, except one little ewe lamb which he had bought and nourished; and it grew up together with him and with his children. It ate of his own food and drank from his own cup and lay in his bosom; and it was like a daughter to him.
>
> And a traveler came to the rich man, who refused to take from his own flock and from his own herd to prepare one for the wayfaring man who had come to him; but he took the poor man's lamb and prepared it for the man who had come to him."

When David heard the prophet's story, he became so angry that he said, "As the Lord lives, the man who has done this shall surely die! And he shall restore fourfold for the lamb, because he did this thing and because he had no pity" (vv. 5,6). In verse 7, we read Nathan's response to David: "*You* are the man."

David had taken Bathsheba from Uriah, and David had committed adultery with her. He then sent a letter to have Uriah killed. And God said, in essence, "You have stolen something that was not yours." God led the prophet Nathan to confront David with this truth. And in Second Samuel 12:13, we see the heart of David *and* the heart of the Lord.

> So David said to Nathan, "I have sinned against the Lord." And Nathan said to David, "The Lord also has put away your sin; you shall not die."

The Power of Forgiveness, Grace, and Mercy

Why are we going into so much detail about David and Bathsheba's great sin? Because God put it away! God didn't hold on to David's sin so He could bring it out before him again or make him pay for it. No, the Bible says God "put away" David's sin.

God put away Bathsheba's sin as well. After David and Bathsheba's first child died, they had a second child whom they named Solomon, which means "beloved of the Lord." During his lifetime, Solomon became the king of Israel and the richest and wisest man in the world. God wasn't looking for ways to punish Bathsheba and David — He wanted to *bless* Bathsheba and David. *That's the powerful forgiveness of our God!*

It is human nature to look at those who have committed what we deem as "great sin," such as murder or adultery, and say, "I know that God has forgiven them, but their life will never be restored. They'll never really have the blessings of God." But that is a lie from the devil! God's grace and mercy were so great upon David and Bathsheba that He said, in essence, "I have put this sin behind Me, and I'm going to bless you with a great son named Solomon. He's going to be a great king and the wisest and richest man on the earth."

And what does this story of redemption say to us? It says that the wisdom and instruction found in Proverbs 31 was written by a woman who had tremendous gratitude toward God for His forgiveness.

The Prayer of True Repentance

God's forgiveness and our true repentance go hand in hand. When David repented and prayed for God to forgive him, he didn't just say, "I'm sorry. I'll do better next time." Psalm 51:1-8 declares David's powerful, heartfelt prayer after he was confronted with his sin by Nathan.

> **Have mercy upon me, O God, according to Your lovingkindness; according to the multitude of Your tender mercies, blot out my transgressions. Wash me thoroughly from my iniquity, and cleanse me from my sin.**
>
> **For I acknowledge my transgressions, and my sin is always before me. Against You, You only, have I sinned, and**

> done this evil in Your sight — that You may be found just when You speak, and blameless when You judge.
>
> Behold, I was brought forth in iniquity, and in sin my mother conceived me. Behold, You desire truth in the inward parts, and in the hidden part You will make me to know wisdom.
>
> Purge me with hyssop, and I shall be clean; wash me, and I shall be whiter than snow. Make me hear joy and gladness, that the bones You have broken may rejoice.

David believed God would do exactly what He said He would do. In God's great forgiveness, He put David's sin behind him, and He blessed David. The Bible even calls David a man after God's own heart (*see* 1 Samuel 13:14). The Bible also tells us that Jesus is a descendant of David — and so is Bathsheba (*see* Matthew 1:6). That's the mercy of God!

Proverbs 31 was written by a woman who knew *redemption*; a woman who knew *the forgiveness of God*. Bathsheba could have focused on her sin, but she repented. And through God's forgiveness, she received His goodness into her life! She didn't let her past mistakes ruin her life. She even came into a position where her instructions on how to be a virtuous woman could be shared with other women for thousands of years!

He Became Sin for a Divine Purpose

Bathsheba's story exemplifies the power of God's forgiveness. He can take a terrible situation, mess, mistake, or sin, and give us a beautiful life and abundant blessings after it. He can still use us for the Kingdom of God. When we truly repent, we are made completely clean of that sin. God's will is that not even the tiniest bit of residue of that sin would continue to linger in our lives. He desires that we be free of it forever.

Second Corinthians 5:21 says, "For He made Him who knew no sin to be sin for us, that we might become the righteousness of God in Him." Jesus didn't just forgive our sin — Jesus *became* our sin. There was never a moment in history like that moment when Jesus was on the Cross. It was such a horrible sight that the Bible says God couldn't even look on Him and man despised Him (*see* Isaiah 53:3). Jesus went to the Cross so that when we confess our sins before God and repent, His cleansing power comes to restore us and make us as if we've never sinned. This is the cleansing power that Bathsheba experienced!

What a testimony Bathsheba's story is to us — a woman who was an adulteress, an accomplice to murder, a deceiver, and a liar to a whole nation. But when she repented, God elevated her to such a place of restoration and confidence that she could see herself as one who could teach her son how to be a godly king. And through the ages, she has stood out as a model of womanhood by giving us these precious verses of scripture in Proverbs 31.

Limitless Possibilities Through a God Who Loves and Forgives

Instead of looking at Proverbs 31 as an impossible standard of achievement, we can see in its words a woman who received complete forgiveness from God. He forgave her sin and blessed her with an amazing son and future king, Solomon. And through her, He gave us this amazing passage of scripture.

This is the result of forgiveness that was extended to men and women during Old Testament times — before grace and mercy were purchased for us on the Cross. Just think of what He can do with us as we confess our sin and repent through the mighty blood of Jesus! The possibilities are limitless because we have received His life — a life so abundant, a life without limits, and joy unspeakable. His love is without condition, and He has placed that love and peace in our hearts! *This* is how we can look at the teachings in Proverbs 31 — not as a threat of failure if we don't do everything right but as a great testimony of a woman who was forgiven much.

Bathsheba took hold of that new identity as one forgiven, redeemed, and restored. She became a confident teacher to her son, training him up to be a mighty man of God, and a teacher to countless generations of females, exhorting them — *you and me* — to be virtuous women.

STUDY QUESTIONS

> Be diligent to present yourself approved to God, a worker who does not need to be ashamed, rightly dividing the word of truth.
> — 2 Timothy 2:15

1. Memorize Ephesians 4:31 and 32. (Denise says these verses almost every day of her life.)

Let all bitterness, wrath, anger, clamor, and evil speaking be put away from you, with all malice. And be kind to one another, tenderhearted, forgiving one another, even as God in Christ forgave you.

2. "If we confess our sins, He is faithful and just to forgive us our sins and to cleanse us from all unrighteousness" (1 John 1:9). Thank God for the gift of forgiveness! What does First John 1:9 tell us *our* part is in receiving forgiveness and cleansing from all unrighteousness?
3. If you received Jesus as your Lord, the debt of sin no longer exists for you. The debt is erased because of Jesus' finished work on the Cross. Take a moment to remind yourself of this glorious truth. Read Colossians 1:14; Isaiah 53:4 and 5; Hebrews 9:12; and First Peter 1:18 and 19.

PRACTICAL APPLICATION

But be doers of the word,
and not hearers only, deceiving yourselves.
—James 1:22

1. Luke 6:37 says, "Judge not, and you shall not be judged. Condemn not, and you shall not be condemned. Forgive, and you will be forgiven." Are you harboring unforgiveness in your heart against someone — your husband, your child, or a friend? Ask that person to forgive you and release that person by forgiving him or her. If a relationship has been strained, ask that other person to forgive you.
2. Read Matthew 7:1-5 and ask God to show you if you have any judgmental attitudes in your heart.

   Judge not, that you be not judged. For with what judgment you judge, you will be judged; and with the measure you use, it will be measured back to you. And why do you look at the speck in your brother's eye, but do not consider the plank in your own eye? Or how can you say to your brother, 'Let me remove the speck from your eye'; and look, a plank is in your own eye? Hypocrite! First remove the plank from your own eye, and then you will see clearly to remove the speck from your brother's eye.

LESSON 2

TOPIC
What Can Forgiveness Do for the Guilty?

SCRIPTURES
1. **Proverbs 31:1-9** — The words of King Lemuel [Solomon], the utterance which his mother taught him: What, my son? And what, son of my womb? And what, son of my vows? Do not give your strength to women, nor your ways to that which destroys kings. It is not for kings, O Lemuel, it is not for kings to drink wine, nor for princes intoxicating drink; lest they drink and forget the law, and pervert the justice of all the afflicted. Give strong drink to him who is perishing, and wine to those who are bitter of heart. Let him drink and forget his poverty, and remember his misery no more. Open your mouth for the speechless, in the cause of all who are appointed to die. Open your mouth, judge righteously, and plead the cause of the poor and needy.
2. **Matthew 26:44,45** (*KJV*) — And he left them, and went away again, and prayed the third time, saying the same words. Then cometh he to his disciples, and saith unto them, Sleep on now, and take your rest: behold, the hour is at hand, and the Son of man is betrayed into the hands of sinners.

SYNOPSIS
Proverbs 31 begins with several life lessons that Solomon remembers his mother, Bathsheba, imparted to him. These verses reveal how crucial it is for mothers to take on the responsibility to teach their children what they need to know to live a godly life. By finding the courage to teach our children how to stay pure, make good decisions, and be a positive influence on others, we set them up for success throughout their lives.

The emphasis of this lesson:

As parents and grandparents, it is imperative that we share godly principles and life lessons with our children. We must rise up and take the

precious time we have with them to speak the truth in love, so they may do well all their days and avoid the enemy's traps.

Raising Godly Children Requires Godly Parenting

In the previous lesson, we considered the great forgiveness that God extended to David and Bathsheba. Many commentators say that she is the one who wrote Proverbs 31, which contains her instructions to Solomon, her son. This woman — who was an adulterer, accomplice to a murder, and a deceiver — received God's forgiveness, and He elevated her to such a high position that we have her teachings and advice to glean from today. Let's begin our study by looking at Proverbs 31:1 and 2, which says:

> **The words of King Lemuel, the utterance which his mother taught him: What, my son? And what, son of my womb? And what, son of my vows?**

It is amazing to see these instructions from a mother to her son. Her words, "What, son of my womb? And what, son of my vows?" reveal that she was taking seriously the responsibility for raising her son to be a godly man. How could she *not* teach him? She gave birth to him, and she was honoring the vows she made before God and to her son by teaching and instructing him. Bathsheba spoke from an open heart to her son, and we can learn a great deal from her about raising our children in the ways of the Lord.

Principle One: Teach the Value of Staying Pure

The first lesson Bathsheba shared with Solomon is found in Proverbs 31:3, which says, "Do not give your strength to women, nor your ways to that which destroys kings." In this verse, Bathsheba was speaking about sex. It may seem embarrassing to think about giving our children instruction on what is and what is not appropriate when it comes to sex, but Bathsheba did not shy away from addressing this sensitive but important topic.

Consider this: Who is the most fitted for the job of instructing your child and giving them godly admonition on the intimate subjects of sexual purity? As a parent, would you want your child to find out on the street about sexual matters? Or from their friends? In a classroom? Who is better suited to give your children instruction like this than *you*, their loving parent? Bathsheba took that responsibility upon herself, and she taught

Solomon that he should not give himself casually to women, because to do so would be giving up his strength.

When men give themselves to many women, it steals their strength. They may not realize this is happening; they may think they are simply having a good time. But this immoral behavior is stealing their very strength. If you are a parent or grandparent caring for your children or grandchildren, you need to instruct them in the wisdom of Proverbs 31, just as Bathsheba instructed Solomon. It is *your* responsibility to instruct them on how very important it is to keep themselves pure.

Principle Two: Teach the Benefits of Good Judgment

The next lesson Bathsheba addressed with her son, Solomon, concerned the subject of the consumption of alcohol. In Proverbs 31:4 and 5, Bathsheba said, "…It is not for kings to drink wine, nor for princes intoxicating drink; lest they drink and forget the law, and pervert the justice of all the afflicted." From her choice of words, we can discern that she was warning him against allowing alcohol to take over his judgment. Your child's judgment is very important to his or her future and to his or her future success.

When people are under the influence of drugs or alcohol, it affects their judgment; they make poor decisions. In her program, Denise shared the story of a man who decided to go drinking with his friends. He didn't realize it, but alcohol was taking hold of him. He didn't have control of alcohol; alcohol had control of him. Sadly, he ended up in a situation where he got angry and killed somebody because of the influence that alcohol had on his thinking.

As parents, we don't want that to happen to our children. We want them to be equipped with godly instruction — such as the wisdom found in Proverbs 31 — so they are fully aware that drinking alcohol or taking drugs are not wise choices. And this is what Bathsheba did as she taught Solomon godly life principles. She protected what was precious to her and precious in her child.

Guard What Is Precious in Your Child

What is precious in your child? One thing that's precious in your child is their judgment — their ability to know right from wrong. As parents, we can raise our children in such a way that when they grow up they become responsible adults. We can guide them so that they learn to have confidence, exercise authority over themselves, and have the boldness to address what is right and what is wrong.

When people use and abuse alcohol and drugs, it affects their perception, and it can cause great damage to their life. In her program, Denise shared her personal experience of ministering monthly at a drug and alcohol hospital in Moscow. The people there had become so addicted to drugs or alcohol (or both) that they couldn't live without it. She said:

> I looked into the eyes of mothers who had lost their children. Why did they lose their children? Because these mothers were addicted to drugs and not capable of raising their children. So somebody took their children to protect them.
>
> I looked into the eyes of young, 16-year-old girls who were absolutely drug-addicted. They looked at me and said, "I hear what you're saying about Jesus. Can He help me? Can He help me get off these drugs? Can He really make a change in my life?" You see, the drugs had control over them. They didn't have control over the drugs.

What a terrible place to be in! As parents, we need to warn and teach our children against the dangers of alcohol and drugs, so they can live godly lives and be free of anything that would keep them from making wise decisions and being successful.

Principle Three: Teach Your Child To Make a Difference

After instructing her son concerning the pitfalls of women and wine, Bathsheba spoke to her son about having mercy upon others. In Proverbs 31:8 and 9, she said, "Open your mouth for the speechless, in the cause of all who are appointed to die. Open your mouth, judge righteously, and plead the cause of the poor and needy."

Bathsheba was counseling her son to extend mercy, understanding, and care to those who couldn't care for themselves. She instructed him to speak up on behalf of those who could not speak up for themselves. She reminded him that he had influence because of his authority, and that he had the power to open his mouth and defend the cause of the poor and the needy.

This is so important! As a godly mother, Bathsheba was teaching her son to have a tender heart and use his influence to help others. Likewise, we need to teach our children and our grandchildren to live as the influencers that they are, rather than being influenced by those around them. Our sons and daughters can make a difference in someone else's life by being merciful and tender-hearted and speaking up for those who can't speak up for themselves.

Accept the Responsibility To Teach Your Children

If Bathsheba was teaching these principles to her son, shouldn't we take cues from her about teaching our own children these powerful lessons? Just as she did, we should warn our sons and daughters about the dangers of drugs and alcohol, instruct them about the importance of purity, and impress upon them that their body doesn't belong to anyone but the person they marry. We ought to teach them to have mercy upon those in need and to use their voice to help others.

There may be some obstacles that you must overcome to be able to speak to your child so candidly. You may be afraid to be that honest, that bold, and that clear with your child about some of these life lessons. You may have never thought about having to fill this role for your son or daughter. Sometimes people look to the father or grandfather to teach their children these things, but he may not take it upon himself to do so. He may be too busy or working too hard. His mind may be so focused on succeeding at work that he's not thinking about instructing his children.

You may not have known you were supposed to teach your children in this way, and you may have never heard of the powerful life lessons in Proverbs 31. But now you *do* know. Praise God! Just as Bathsheba took it upon herself to share these principles with her son, those of us who are mothers and grandmothers can take it upon ourselves to watch over our children and impart these powerful principles to them.

Guide Your Children Away From Paths of Danger

By teaching your child these biblical life lessons, you can help them avoid great danger. In her program, Denise shared a powerful, heart-wrenching example of what can happen when you ignore Biblical wisdom.

> I heard about a young person — about 16 or 17 years old — who was drinking while driving. He was driving 90 miles per hour on

the wrong side of the road when he collided with another vehicle. The crash killed the other male driver and injured the female passenger — the man's wife. They were simply driving home from work. Why did that tragedy happen? Because that young person foolishly chose to drink and then drive — and that choice killed a man.

Alcohol and drugs are sometimes considered "glamorous" or "cool." Your children may hear others say, "Oh, you haven't experienced that yet? You need to widen your horizons." As mothers, we need to teach our children that these are lies from the devil that are intended to take them down the wrong path. Words of truth need to come out of our mouths and into our children's ears, so they can avoid the path of danger.

Your Child Wants Your Instruction

As a mother, you have so many responsibilities! You have your children, and perhaps you have a husband, a house, and a job. You may have an elderly parent you're responsible for too. Or you may be a single parent who needs to pay the bills *while* caring for your children. The cares of life may have you feeling so overwhelmed that you don't know how in the world you can find the time to teach your children such vital truths and life lessons.

The encouraging word for you is that it doesn't take long to take your child aside and say, "Sweetheart, I need to teach you some very important things. I want you to know from my heart what I believe is good for you and what I believe is bad for you."

You may think your child is not going to listen to you. That's wrong! Children *want* instruction. They *desire* borders and boundaries. Borders aren't bondage — they create the safety that your son or daughter needs. Your child *wants* to hear from you. As a parent, you have the influence and the power to teach your child well.

The good news is that you don't have to be perfect to give wise instruction. Remember Bathsheba? She was far from perfect, but she was greatly forgiven by God. She flourished under His forgiveness and stood with confidence as she imparted these valuable lessons to her son. And we can too!

Don't Take Time With Your Child for Granted

In a chapter of her book *Do You Know What Time It Is?*, Denise focuses on several verses in Matthew 26. In that passage of Scripture, Jesus was praying in the Garden of Gethsemane. He had asked the disciples to pray with Him, but when He returned, He found them sleeping. Jesus, again, asked the disciples to keep watch and pray. He withdrew to pray, but when He came back to them a second time, again, they had fallen asleep. Matthew 26:44 and 45 in the *King James Version* tells us:

> **And he left them, and went away again, and prayed the third time, saying the same words. Then cometh he to his disciples, and saith unto them, Sleep on now, and take your rest: behold, the hour is at hand, and the Son of man is betrayed into the hands of sinners.**

Jesus goes on to say, "Rise, let us be going. See, My betrayer is at hand" (Matthew 26:46). Do you think His disciples knew while they were taking their nap that Jesus was about to be betrayed by Judas, arrested, scourged by the Romans, and hung on a cruel cross to die for the sins of the world? Of course, they didn't. They probably thought, *I know Jesus asked me to pray, but I'm really sleepy, so I'm going to take a little nap. He'll be there after I wake up.*

Have you ever taken a loved one for granted? In her program, Denise shared the story of a woman who told her, "I didn't treat my husband right. I didn't love him like I should have. Then one day I received a phone call and learned he was killed in a car accident. He died instantly. I had had the chance to love him. I had had the chance to tell him that I loved him and treat him well, but now my chance was gone."

Likewise, the disciples had the chance to pray with Jesus, but then their chance was gone.

Take Time To Impart Godly Wisdom to Your Children

These examples remind us that we can't take for granted the time we have with our children and grandchildren. We must not ignore or delay sharing the wisdom we have. We don't want our children to endanger themselves by using drugs or alcohol or engaging in sexual relationships before they're married. So we must open our mouth and warn our children that they do not want to go in the direction of the world — and we must do it while we have the opportunity.

You have a limited time to impart godly wisdom to your children and grandchildren — the sliver of time when their young heart and ears are open to you. But there comes a time when their ears and heart are not as open. Their life is becoming *their* life, and they're too busy. And you no longer have the precious time of impartation with them that you once did. So take the time you have now and use it well. Please don't take it for granted. (For more information on this powerful topic, read Denise's thought-provoking book, *Do You Know What Time It Is?*)

Give the instructions you have to your children, your grandchildren, and those who will listen to you because the clock is ticking! Time is moving — it's not stopping. And the window of opportunity to share your pearls of wisdom may soon be closed.

May you have the courage you need to speak with love and tenderness to those who need the precious lessons in your heart, to warn them, and to help them. In Jesus' name. Amen.

STUDY QUESTIONS

Be diligent to present yourself approved to God, a worker who does not need to be ashamed, rightly dividing the word of truth.
— 2 Timothy 2:15

1. Read Proverbs 31:1-9. What are the three nuggets of wisdom Bathsheba gave to her son, King David, to help him rule with integrity?
2. "And you, fathers, do not provoke your children to wrath, but bring them up in the training and admonition of the Lord" (Ephesians 6:4). In your own words, what does it mean to "bring up your children in the training and admonition of the Lord"?

PRACTICAL APPLICATION

But be doers of the word, and not hearers only, deceiving yourselves.
—James 1:22

1. If you could offer only three wise principles to your children or a young friends, what words of wisdom would you share with them?
2. Were you raised by parents or guardians who imparted godly wisdom to you? If so, how did it affect your transition into adulthood? If not, what choices did you make to set yourself on a path that would honor God? If you are a parent in the midst of raising your children, what steps are you taking to "train up your child in the way they should go"? (*See* Proverbs 22:6.)
3. Take a quick inventory: Do you read your Bible daily? Do your children see you reading your Bible daily? Do they hear you pray? Do they see your consistency in going to church and serving the Lord with your talents? Do you walk in integrity before your children and others? Realize your children are watching you, and God has His eyes on you too. If there are any areas of your life that don't line up with the Word of God, ask the Lord to forgive you for these areas of inconsistency, purpose in your heart to change those areas to align your life with the Word, and live as an example before your children.

LESSON 3

TOPIC

'Help! I'm Not Perfect and Neither Is My Spouse!'

SCRIPTURES

1. **Proverbs 31:11,12** — The heart of her husband safely trusts her; so he will have no lack of gain. She does him good and not evil all the days of her life.
2. **Proverbs 14:1** — The wise woman builds her house, but the foolish pulls it down with her hands.
3. **Ephesians 5:33** — Nevertheless let each one of you in particular so love his own wife as himself, and let the wife see that she respects her husband.

4. **Isaiah 53:5** — But He was wounded for our transgressions, He was bruised for our iniquities; the chastisement for our peace was upon Him, and by His stripes we are healed.

SYNOPSIS

As we continue our study on the Proverbs 31 woman, it's important to keep in mind that these verses of Scripture are intended *not* as an impossibly high standard that no one can reach, but rather as an inspiration of what *is* possible in our lives. Just as Bathsheba was imperfect and yet was forgiven and blessed by the Lord, so are we imperfect — yet we can be blessed as well when we turn to God. This concept is vital in marriage because our husbands are not perfect either. Rather than criticizing or placing blame, we should respect them, accept them for who they are, and let God's wisdom guide us. In this way, we can build up our marriage and see the door opened for us and our spouse to change and grow.

The emphasis of this lesson:

The wisdom of Proverbs 31 is a reminder of what is possible in our marriage when we trust the Lord and let His wisdom guide us in our relationship. As we respect our husbands, accept them for who they are, and act on God's guidance, we open up a path for change — in God's timing.

Godly Wisdom Benefits Every Woman

The Proverbs 31 woman has so many positive attributes that she may seem as if she's perfect, and we can sometimes judge ourselves harshly when we compare ourselves to her. As we read Proverbs 31, we may say to ourselves, "I'm not achieving *this* verse — I'm only able to attain *that* verse sometimes." And as a result, we may feel that we're not measuring up.

Keep in mind, according to tradition, Proverbs 31 was written by Bathsheba and contains her wisdom and instruction to her son, King Solomon. Bathsheba was not criticizing us or judging us; her words were not written to raise a standard so high that no one could reach it. Remember, she herself was an adulteress, an accomplice to a murder, a liar, and a deceiver to a whole nation.

But God forgave Bathsheba, and He elevated her to such a position of confidence and security that she taught her son Solomon and trained him up in the way he should go. She imparted to him how he should think about drinking, about giving his strength to women, and about having a merciful heart toward people who can't speak up for themselves. And then Bathsheba began to teach Solomon about the qualities he should look for in a wife.

In Proverbs 31:11 and 12, Bathsheba said of a good wife, "The heart of her husband safely trusts her; so he will have no lack of gain. She does him good and not evil all the days of her life." In this passage, Bathsheba was magnifying the qualities of a godly wife, but these verses contain amazing instruction for any woman who is looking for guidance on how she can build up her house. Single or married, these teachings will help you build up the relationships you have.

The Myth of Perfection

In her program, Denise shared how, as a little girl, she was enamored with the story of Cinderella. Like many little girls, Denise watched the fairy tale many times, imagining that it would be *her* story. Denise said,

> I watched that fairy tale over and over again, visualizing myself as Cinderella, and dreaming that Prince Charming was going to come down the stairs to the ballroom, look into my eyes, and sweep me off my feet. And we would live happily ever after. I've been married for over 40 years, and I'm not sure I would say I've been a "Cinderella," but I'll say that I've married Prince Charming. But let me tell you this; life has a way of knocking the crown off Cinderella *and* Prince Charming — because people are not perfect.

None of us are perfect — not your husband, not the people around you, and not you. And the situations we find ourselves in are not perfect either. We live in a fallen world, and things happen; things can go amiss. Sometimes we can bring great hurt to one another, especially in a husband-and-wife relationship. It can seem like Cinderella disappeared and took her happily-ever-after ending with her! How can we get her back? (For more on this topic, read Denise's down-to-earth, encouraging book, *Who Stole Cinderella?*)

Build Up Your House — Don't Tear It Down

As we spend time searching the Bible for examples of godly women, we can see great promise, instruction, and encouragement in it for us. Throughout His Word, God is saying that while we might have problems in our house, *we* are the builders. Proverbs 14:1 says, "The wise woman builds her house, but the foolish pulls it down with her hands." Ultimately, *we* are responsible for what happens in our home. We can either gain wisdom and choose to build up our house, or we can ignore wisdom and be foolish and tear it down.

It is with our own hands — the wisdom we gain, the effort we put forth, and being intentional about seeking the Lord — that we can learn how to build up our house and not tear it down. How do we do this? It begins with gaining wisdom. And a part of being wise is *not blaming the other person*. This is so important to learn because we often want to do the opposite — blame the other person in the relationship. Many people say to themselves, *If only my spouse would change, then our marriage would be perfect*.

But there is a big problem with that thinking. We must realize that criticizing our husband, trying to teach him things, complaining, and nagging all the time will not have a positive effect on him. It doesn't encourage him to change. We can't continue to point fingers and place blame for our problems on others. That approach only leads us to live with a victim mentality, and living that way leads to a very lonely life.

A Marriage Transformed by Godly Wisdom

In her program, Denise shared an example of a woman named Natasha, whose marriage was transformed as she learned to walk in godly wisdom toward her husband. She came into church one day for a women's ministry meeting, and everyone noticed how she entered the room like a princess. When they asked her what was going on, she began to share her story.

Natasha explained that she was raised by a mother who was an abusive alcoholic. The abuse she experienced was so devastating that it caused her many psychological and physical problems. By the time she was 21 years old, she was paralyzed and in a wheelchair, and she had no idea what to do with her life. Some people even told her that she should just die because of the hopeless situation she was in. But Natasha had hope in her heart.

At that time, a bold Christian woman lived next door to Natasha, and the Holy Spirit told her to go to Natasha's home. So she went to Natasha's home and knocked. When the door opened, she saw Natasha in the wheelchair. Following the Holy Spirit's instructions, the Christian woman ministered to her, and Natasha was completely healed. But Natasha didn't give her life to Jesus at that time. Instead, she began living with a man who was an alcoholic. He became abusive in his speech, cursing her, and she became hurt and wounded on the inside. As she checked off on the calendar each day that he came home drunk, she developed resentment and bitterness in her heart.

One day, someone invited Natasha to church. There, she gave her life to Jesus, and she asked Him, "Lord, what do I do about this man that I'm living with?" He told her, "I don't want you to leave him, but you can't sleep with him anymore." So she obeyed the Holy Spirit and moved into another room. Then she asked the Lord what to do next, and the Holy Spirit said, "When he comes home tonight, I want you to have on your very best dress. I want you to fix his most favorite food, and when he comes through that door, I want you to put your arms around him, put your hands on his face, and say, 'Oh my love, you've come home.'"

Around midnight, the man came home, and Natasha opened the door wearing a beautiful dress. He could smell the food in the kitchen. He was drunk, and he was rude, but she put her hands on his face and said, "Oh my love, you've come home." The man stood there for two hours because he was so shocked.

Natasha had received this instruction from the Lord, and He didn't tell her to stop. So every night for two years, she continued to greet this man by putting on a beautiful dress, preparing his favorite food, placing her hands on his face, and saying, "Oh my love, you've come home."

It was the hardest thing Natasha had ever done in her life. It took a lot of prayer and fasting too. But this man began to change. He quit drinking and got a job. They got married and he adopted their daughter. Natasha told everyone, "Do you want to know why I walked in here like a princess? Every day when I leave my home, my husband looks at me very tenderly and says, 'I pray for you to have a great day. I love you, my princess.'"

Respect Your Husband by Accepting Him as He Is

Consider this: If Natasha had criticized this man, cursed at him, or tried to tell him what to do, would it have helped? If she had complained all the time and nagged him, would he have changed? Not likely. They probably would not have stayed together, and their little girl would not have had a relationship with her father. But Natasha used a tool that is necessary when *building* a home — accepting your spouse as he is and showing him respect.

Ephesians 5:33 says, "Nevertheless let each one of you in particular so love his own wife as himself, and let the wife see that she respects her husband." In marriage, the husband is to love his wife as himself, and the wife is to respect her husband. Yes, the husband must do his part, but the wife must do her part as well — respecting her husband and accepting him as he is.

Please note: Respecting and accepting your husband does NOT mean that you should accept abuse — such as physical or sexual abuse — of yourself or your children. If you or your children are in an unsafe situation, please seek professional or ministerial help immediately.

It may be difficult for you to respect your husband if he cusses or drinks. Maybe he works too many hours or doesn't go to church with you. Maybe he won't talk to you, never does anything around the house, and doesn't spend time with the children. The list can go on and on, but choosing to build up your home by accepting him is a powerful thing. By doing so, you open a path for the presence of Heaven to come into your home.

Natasha's husband didn't change because she criticized or nagged him, or because she cursed and screamed at him. He didn't change because she ignored him or wouldn't speak to him. She accepted him as he was, and she respected him for who he was. She prayed for him, and he changed because he received the unconditional love of God through her.

Begin the Process of Change by Looking at Yourself

Have you ever been around somebody who wanted you to change, and they made sure you knew it? They rarely said, "Good job" or "Thank you." All they did was criticize you, and you just knew by their words and actions that you were not accepted. As wives, we can make that same mistake — little by little, day by day, month by month, year by year

— building a wall between ourselves and our husbands with our harsh words and stern judgments; building a wall but tearing down the house.

You may think in your heart toward your husband, *I would never do what you just did. I would never speak to you the way you just spoke to me. Why can't you be more like me? Why can't you be more like God? Why can't you be more like my father?* We may even let these words come out of our mouth — and then we don't understand why our husband doesn't want to talk to us. The issue is that we have to look at ourselves *first*.

If we ever want our marriage to change, we must first consider ourselves and ask, *What can I do differently? What am I doing that is causing problems in my marriage? What is inside my heart toward my husband?* We must ask these questions, and then we have to take them to the Cross. Oh, the power of the Cross!

Isaiah 53:5 says, "But He was wounded for our transgressions, He was bruised for our iniquities; the chastisement for our peace was upon Him, and by His stripes we are healed." Anything that would take our peace was put on Jesus at the Cross. When we're wounded and can't find that place of peace, we can go to Jesus. He took those wounds in our hearts upon Himself. He took the bruises in our soul on Himself. He took the pain and the hurt, and He destroyed its power so that it could not wrap itself around us and put us in an emotional prison for the rest of our life. That's the power of the Cross!

When you're honest with God about your feelings toward your husband and your desire to see your husband change, God can come into your situation and transform *you* with the truth of His Word. And as He leads you by His Holy Spirit to a place where you can respect your husband and accept him for who he is, God can begin to bring about a transformation in your marriage.

STUDY QUESTIONS

**Be diligent to present yourself approved to God, a worker who does not need to be ashamed, rightly dividing the word of truth.
— 2 Timothy 2:15**

1. The Word of God is the best blueprint for how to build a godly home. According to Proverbs 24:3; Psalm 127:1; Proverbs 24:27;

Matthew 18:19,20; Hebrews 10:25; Deuteronomy 6:5-9; and Proverbs 22:6, what does this construction effort look like?
2. Marriage is hard work. What are a few ways a spouse can "work" to strengthen the marriage? (*Consider* Ephesians 4:32, Ephesians 4:2, and Galatians 6:2.)

PRACTICAL APPLICATION

**But be doers of the word,
and not hearers only, deceiving yourselves.
—James 1:22**

1. Ephesians 5:33 admonishes, "Nevertheless let each one of you in particular so love his own wife as himself, and let the wife see that she respects her husband." What are some practical ways a man can love his wife? What are some tangible ways a wife can show respect to her husband?
2. Is your spouse a good employee at work? Is he kind and compassionate? Is he a good son? A good father? Write down the three best qualities of your husband. This week, bring at least one of these attributes to your husband's attention and sincerely thank him for it.
3. In the program, Denise admonished us to ask ourselves, *Do I hang on to the sins of the past that my husband committed against me?* If you've struggled with unforgiveness, take time to read Acts 7:54-60 concerning the martyrdom of Stephen and his forgiveness of those stoning him. Rather than trying to change your husband, forgive him quickly, and refuse to hold on to offense. Purpose in your heart to immediately release your husband at the moment of offense and notice how freeing it is to live with this mindset!

LESSON 4

TOPIC
'How Can I Be Nice to a Difficult Husband?'

SCRIPTURES
1. **Proverbs 31:11,12** — The heart of her husband safely trusts her; so he will have no lack of gain. She does him good and not evil all the days of her life.
2. **John 14:26** — But the Helper, the Holy Spirit, whom the Father will send in My name, He will teach you all things, and bring to your remembrance all things that I said to you.
3. **Matthew 11:28-30** — "Come to Me, all you who labor and are heavy laden, and I will give you rest. Take My yoke upon you and learn from Me, for I am gentle and lowly in heart, and you will find rest for your souls. For My yoke is easy and My burden is light."
4. **Psalm 119:105** — Your word is a lamp to my feet and a light to my path.

SYNOPSIS
The Bible instructs the godly wife to do good and not evil toward her husband; this is her commitment in marriage. Yet it is not always easy to live this way because we live in a fallen world and none of us is perfect. Thankfully, God has given us the Holy Spirit who lives inside us as our Helper — and He can provide us with the guidance we need to be successful in fulfilling the instructions of Proverbs 31. As we open our hearts honestly before the Lord and ask for His help, the Holy Spirit will instruct us on how to successfully handle the challenges of marriage.

The emphasis of this lesson:

No matter what challenges arise in our marriage or what we are facing in our relationship with our spouse, we are to always measure our actions, words, and thoughts against the truth of God's Word — His measuring stick for our lives. And through the work of the Holy Spirit,

our Helper, we are empowered to successfully live out the Word as godly wives.

As we continue our study of Proverbs 31, we can be encouraged by God's goodness and mercy toward us. Bathsheba, whom many scholars credit as the one the Holy Spirit used to pen this chapter of the Bible, was not a perfect woman. But through God's grace and Bathsheba's repentance, God forgave her, and He lifted her to such a high position that thousands of years later, people continue to study her writings to learn about living a virtuous life.

Have you ever heard someone say if you commit a great sin that you will have to pay for that sin the rest of your life, your life will never be the same, and God will never use you the way He did before? That's a lie from the enemy! When Jesus forgives, the Bible says He separates our sin as far from us as the east is from the west (*see* Psalm 103:12). Jesus casts that sin away from us because of His great love and compassion. This is what He did for Bathsheba. Not only did He lift her up, but He lifted her to the place of a great teacher, which is why we're studying her words of wisdom.

A Place of Comfort and Trust

In Proverbs 31, we find Bathsheba's instructions to her son, Solomon, on the qualities he should look for in a wife. Proverbs 31:11 says of this godly woman, "The heart of her husband safely trusts her; so he will have no lack of gain." What powerful words of instruction to help us build up our house and have a strong marriage!

This verse begins, "The heart of her husband safely trusts her...." A husband should find a place of safety, trust, and comfort from his wife. Picture a very cold, wintery day, and a husband comes into his home. There's a warm fire and a cup of hot tea or coffee awaiting him — something warm, something welcoming. This home is a place of safety for him on this cold day. Likewise, a wife should be a place of comfort and safety to her husband, so he doesn't need to guard his heart but rather is confident that he can trust her with his heart.

A virtuous wife is a powerful and wise woman who provides a place of safety, trust, and comfort for her husband, but it's not always easy. We're imperfect women married to imperfect husbands, and we don't live in a perfect world. There will be pain and problems. But through the power of the Holy Spirit and the wisdom of His Word, we can find places where we can be a comfort to our husband. We can build a home and a marriage in which our husband can find warmth and create a place where he wants to *run to* rather than *run from*.

A Place That Empowers Safety and Success

Why do we need to create a place of safety and trust that will ensure our husband doesn't have to guard his heart from the pain we might cause him? The second half of Proverbs 31:11 gives us the answer. It says, "…So he will have no lack of gain." By creating a place where a husband's heart can be safe, a wife can enable her husband's success and not hinder it.

One statistic says that when husbands and wives warmly kiss each other goodbye, those couples experience 40 percent fewer car accidents than those who leave home having something in their heart against one another. These warm greetings and goodbyes cause our heart to be comforted by our spouse, and they even cause us to be more careful drivers.

We can see the benefits of a husband's trusting heart in the workplace as well. If your husband doesn't have to worry about who he's going to come home to, or whether he is going to have peace and harmony or strife and resentment when he gets home, this scripture says that "he will have no lack of gain." He will be positioned to be more creative and to work harder because he's *not* worried about his home life.

A wise wife will develop a commitment in her heart and in her attitude that she will provide a place of comfort for her husband instead of a place of unrest. By doing so, she will help her husband to do better at work. It may even cause him to get a promotion and make more money! He will have no lack of gain!

A Place of Doing Good and Not Evil

Proverbs 31:12 builds on this idea of creating a place of safety and trust for a husband's heart. Speaking of the godly wife, this verse says, "She does him good and not evil all the days of her life." This is quite a commitment to make, but it is so important for a wife to do so.

Some women might enter into marriage like a fairy tale — like Cinderella and Prince Charming — marrying their best friend, wearing a beautiful white wedding dress, and going on a romantic honeymoon. And this couple may really enjoy each other for two or three years…but then the fairy tale gives way to reality. She may start to see her husband's faults, or he doesn't speak to her as nicely as he once did. They have misunderstandings and it's harder to communicate with one another. Suddenly, the walls seem to be going up as the relationship breaks down, and they find themselves looking for a way to escape. Hopefully, this is not *your* story. However, some statistics state that 30-50 percent of Christian marriages end in divorce. It shouldn't be this way.

When a man and a woman get married, they are making a covenant with one another and God. The commitment they make is *not* that they will stay in the marriage *if* everything goes okay. No! That covenant is about giving of themselves to that other person — for better and for worse, for richer and for poorer, in sickness and in health — until death separates them. It's a *life-long commitment.* And Proverbs 31 shows us that a godly woman and wife will remain committed not only in the good times but at *all* times. She's committed to doing good to her husband and not evil all the days of her life.

In her program, Denise shared a personal story about maintaining the covenant of commitment in a marriage. She said, "I've been married for over 40 years, and when my husband and I got married, we made a commitment to one another and a commitment to God. And we said we would *never, never, never* say the word 'divorce' in our family. Everything hasn't always been perfect. There have been problems and challenges because we live in a fallen world and neither of us is perfect. But even with those challenges, the back door to escape was never opened. The back door of our commitment to one another will always remain closed."

Keep the Back Door Closed

What happens when we "close the back door" and stay dedicated to making our relationship and marriage work? First, it causes us to *seek God*! It leads us to turn to Him and be honest about where we are spiritually, mentally, and emotionally — in every area of our life. When things are not going well or we feel that we don't understand everything that's going on, we can bring those concerns to the Lord and seek Him. In doing so, we're saying, "I'm committed 'until death do us part' to do good to him and not evil." There is such a powerful commitment in these words.

Second, as we stay committed to the relationship and seek God, we can see His measuring stick for our life — the Bible — which acts as our guide when we face challenges with our spouse. In marriage, and any relationship, we can be tempted to become frustrated. We may not like how the other person has acted or what he said. We may feel misunderstood, and we may not want to explain ourselves or seek understanding. Eventually, we may even feel we can take care of ourselves, so we determine that we don't need to stay in the marriage (or relationship) any longer. If we're not careful, we will exalt our own thoughts and emotions and become ensnared by them.

But in the Word of God, we have a measuring stick — a guide for our lives. Temptations may come, and we might even fall for them, like saying words we shouldn't say or doing something we shouldn't do. But even when that happens, we can get back up and return to the measuring stick of God's Word. We can choose, again, that we are going to do good and not evil toward our spouse, and keep the back door closed.

Turn to the Holy Spirit, Your Helper and Guide

How do you successfully live out the wisdom of Proverbs 31:11 and 12 in your relationship with your spouse? You turn to the amazing Teacher and Guide inside you — the Holy Spirit. John 14:26 says, "But the Helper, the Holy Spirit, whom the Father will send in My name, He will teach you all things, and bring to your remembrance all things that I said to you." This is so encouraging!

The Holy Spirit isn't going to just teach you *some* things — He's going to teach you *all* things. When you open your heart and ask the Holy Spirit for help, He will answer you! When you don't know what to do, when you have questions, or when there is division between you and your spouse, you can always call on the Holy Spirit who lives inside you. He is an excellent Helper! He is brilliant and all-knowing, and He wants to teach you everything that will help you in your marriage.

When you open your heart and say, "Help me, Holy Spirit," He comes with help; He comes with answers; He comes to teach you how to handle your relationship. He'll say, in essence, "The next time this happens, don't say that" or "The next time he does this, don't think that. Think and say this instead" or "Your husband means to do well, but he's struggling in this area." That's the Holy Spirit — your Helper — inside you, teaching you which direction to go. He will teach you and guide you. He will help you to control your mouth and change your thoughts.

Our thoughts are incredibly important. If we allow our thoughts to go unchecked, they will say what they want to say about our spouse, and what they say will usually be negative. And if we don't put an end to those negative thoughts, we will start acting on them by closing our heart or behaving rudely or being less patient. We need help keeping our thoughts in line with the Word. We need the Holy Spirit — our Helper.

Receive God's Help in Your Marriage

Jesus said, "Come to Me, all you who labor and are heavy laden, and I will give you rest. Take My yoke upon you and learn from Me, for I am gentle and lowly in heart, and you will find rest for your souls. For My yoke is easy and My burden is light" (Matthew 11:28-30). Do you see His invitation? Jesus is inviting us to *come* to Him. He is so accommodating, and He is so loving.

No matter what you're facing, the Holy Spirit is your Helper, and He is on your side. He's not standing back from you, saying, "You're too dirty. You messed up too much. You struggle too much in this area." No. He's saying, "I'm here to help! Ask Me. The Helper is My name. I want to teach you in this area." If you're struggling in your marriage to do good and stop doing evil, the Holy Spirit is there for you. He is there with open arms, saying to you, "I'm here with My help. Come to Me. I have the wisdom you need. I know all things, and I can teach you." This is the *truth* of what God has for us in our relationships.

The Word of God is our guide — it's a lamp to our feet and a light to our path (*see* Psalm 119:105). So when we find ourselves in a place of not knowing what to do, no matter how dark things look or how lost we feel, His Word is the wisdom, direction, and encouragement we need to keep the back door closed. The Holy Spirit is our Helper. And we can receive God's truth and wisdom to stand strong in our commitment to our marriage, doing good and not evil toward our spouse, all the days of our life.

STUDY QUESTIONS

> Be diligent to present yourself approved to God, a worker
> who does not need to be ashamed, rightly dividing the word of truth.
> — 2 Timothy 2:15

1. Philippians 4:8 says, "…Whatever things are true, whatever things are noble, whatever things are just, whatever things are pure, whatever things are lovely, whatever things are of good report, if there is any virtue and if there is anything praiseworthy — meditate on these things." If you have a thought that is *not* true, noble, just, pure, lovely, of good report, virtuous, and praiseworthy, what should you do with it? (*Consider* Second Corinthians 10:5.)

2. Matthew 11:28 invites you to come unto Him if you are weary, and He will give you rest. His instruction continues, "Take My yoke upon you and learn from Me, for I am gentle and lowly in heart, and you will find rest for your souls. For My yoke is easy and My burden is light" (Matthew 11:29,30). Jesus provides a place where your soul — your mind, your will, and your emotions — can rest. What else does His Word say about restoration and refreshing in Him? (*Consider* Psalm 23:1-3 and Acts 3:19).

PRACTICAL APPLICATION

> **But be doers of the word,
> and not hearers only, deceiving yourselves.**
> — James 1:22

1. "For the weapons of our warfare are not carnal but mighty in God for pulling down strongholds, casting down arguments and every high thing that exalts itself against the knowledge of God, bringing every thought into captivity to the obedience of Christ" (2 Corinthians 10:4,5). This means we are to take every thought captive — capturing every thought and ensuring it lines up with the Word of God. Do you have any thoughts that need to be "taken captive" and "brought to the obedience of Jesus"? Start practicing now by taking that thought(s) captive, refusing to give it any more space in your head, and replacing it with a scripture that brings hope and life.

2. For your eyes only, write a humble affirmation of your acceptance of your husband just *as he is*. Think about God's love and grace in your

own life in spite of your shortcomings. Ask the Father to show you your husband in a new light — the way *He* sees him. Read this affirmation often.

3. Denise spoke in her program about the Holy Spirit and His power inside you. Right now, *at this very moment,* He's your Helper! And an hour from now, He's your Helper. When you drive home from work, He's your Helper. Tonight when you go to bed, He's your Helper. Take a moment and pray because the Helper, the Holy Spirit, is there with you — to help. *Father, I thank You for the Holy Spirit inside me. And Lord, thank You that You're helping me with the problems I'm facing in my relationship. And I thank You for the power of the Holy Spirit and His willingness to teach me and to lead me into truth in every relationship. I thank You for Your presence, Holy Spirit. I will never take it for granted. In Jesus' name. Amen.*

LESSON 5

TOPIC
'To Do' or 'Not To Do' — That Is the Challenge

SCRIPTURES

1. **Proverbs 31:16** — She considers a field and buys it; from her profits she plants a vineyard.
2. **Philippians 1:9,10** — And this I pray, that your love may abound still more and more in knowledge and all discernment, that you may approve the things that are excellent, that you may be sincere and without offense till the day of Christ.
3. **Proverbs 4:20-22** — My son, give attention to my words; incline your ear to my sayings. Do not let them depart from your eyes; keep them in the midst of your heart; for they are life to those who find them, and health to all their flesh.
4. **Proverbs 3:3,4** — Let not mercy and truth forsake you; bind them around your neck, write them on the tablet of your heart, and so find favor and high esteem in the sight of God and man.

SYNOPSIS

As we continue our study of Proverbs 31, we're reminded that it's God's grace and redeeming power that makes it possible for us to receive His favor, just as Bathsheba did. And in Proverbs 31:16, we discover the power of *considering* our thoughts and desires before we act on them so we can make fruitful choices that benefit us and our families. Using God's Word, we can evaluate the many decisions we make every day — whether we are making an investment, deciding how to support our spouse in public, studying the Bible, or believing for healing in our body. As we choose what is vital, excellent, and worthwhile, we will be richly blessed.

The emphasis of this lesson:

God has given us His powerful and healing Word, and He has given us a mind that can consider what we say and do before we speak and act. As we spend time in His Word and ask ourselves questions to weigh and consider our thoughts, we can choose to give our energy to what is vital, excellent, and worthwhile.

The Redeeming Power of the Blood of Jesus Christ

As we've noted before, many scholars agree that Proverbs 31 was penned by Bathsheba, the mother of Solomon. And in previous lessons, we've seen why that's such a miracle! Bathsheba — a woman who was an adulterer, accomplice to a murder, a liar, and a deceiver — repented to the Lord and was raised to such a level that we have been looking to her instruction for thousands of years on how to be a virtuous woman. This miracle displays the marvelous and powerful grace of God to redeem us. And because of His grace, Bathsheba was able to share her wisdom that has helped many marriages!

God's grace is truly amazing. People may really mess up and break their covenant with their spouse by committing adultery. But if someone truly repents to the Lord and begins moving forward in their life with God, we should not judge. We should not say, "It's good that you repented, but I want you to know it's never going to be like it was before." That kind of thinking is a lie from the enemy because we know from the truth of God's Word that the redeeming power of the blood of Jesus Christ can transform us.

Jesus didn't just *take* our sin; He *became* our sin (*see* 2 Corinthians 5:21). The Bible says His appearance was so disfigured and His form so marred beyond human likeness when He went to the Cross that people were appalled and devastated by what they saw (*see* Isaiah 52:14). Why? Because when the Father laid all the shame, all the guilt, and all the hate, murder, lying, stealing, and adultery — *all* our ugly, horrible sin — on His precious Son (*see* Isaiah 53:6), Jesus *became* our sin on the Cross. God turned His face away, unable to look on sin (*see* Isaiah 59:2), as Jesus cried out, "My God, My God, why have You forsaken me?" (Matthew 27:46).

Jesus did that for you! Jesus took that sin and the punishment for it *forever*, so you wouldn't have to spend eternity in hell, separated from your loving Father. He took the scars so sin wouldn't scar *your* life forever. If you've done something wrong, and somebody said to you, "I know you've repented, but you'll never really recover," know that those words are a lie from the devil. If you have said to yourself, "How can God use me after I've messed up so badly?" — know that He can, because He's a redeeming God! We see that redeeming grace in the lives of Bathsheba and King David.

Consider Your Actions Daily

Bathsheba continued her words of wisdom in Proverbs 31:16. It says, "She considers a field and buys it; from her profits she plants a vineyard." Let's look at a very powerful word in this verse — the word "consider." Remember that Bathsheba was describing the type of woman she wanted her son, Solomon, to marry. She wanted him to find a woman who *thought* about her actions.

Every single day of our life we're making decisions, one right after the other: *Will I listen to that thought? No. Will I say that word? No. Will I defend myself? Yes. What will I eat? When will I go to bed? How will I act when I get up in the morning?* We're making decisions all day long. To illustrate this point, Denise shared a personal story from her youth.

> When I was growing up, I had a very melancholy personality. I would wake up, and I wouldn't be in a very good mood. And I would come to the breakfast table and my dad would even say, "Well, here comes the old bear," because I would just drag myself into the kitchen with this sad and serious face. I thought that was just the way I was and that I couldn't change it. But it's not true. I

discovered that I could change it. And if you wake up that way in the morning — like an old bear — you can change it too.

In other words, you can *consider* your actions. You can *decide* how you're going to treat people when you wake up in the morning. You can consider whether you're going to smile at your children and your spouse or avoid them. You can choose whether you are going to carry around the thought, *I'm so tired. It's just another day* or if you are going to give out of your heart to the people you love.

You have the power and ability to consider your actions; you're not a slave to your emotions or mood. *You* get to decide; *you* get to choose. This godly woman in Proverbs 31:16 *considered* what to do before she did it. And likewise, we can consider our actions before we act.

Approve What Is Excellent, Vital, and Worthwhile

In Philippians 1:9 and 10, the apostle Paul prayed, "And this I pray, that your love may abound still more and more in knowledge and all discernment, that you may *approve* the things that are excellent, that you may be sincere and without offense till the day of Christ." The word "approve" in this verse means *to consider* or *to examine*. What's interesting is that this word, translated "approve" in Philippians 1:10, is also a derivative of the very word translated "consider" in Bathsheba's instructions in Proverbs 31:16. So as a wise woman *considers* and *examines* a field before buying it, so should we *consider* and *examine* "the things that are excellent."

The apostle Paul was encouraging the Philippian believers — and us — to *consider* and *examine* what we are giving our life to. What *are* we giving our energy and mind to? Are we giving ourselves over to worry? Is worry excellent? No! Is what we're worrying about a life-or-death situation? Usually not. Is it worth your time to worry? No. And that's just one example of what we can consider and then make a decision about.

Here's another example of *considering* and *examining* before acting. Imagine that you and your husband are out with some friends. Your husband is so excited to tell the story of the fish he caught. He says it was "this big" — indicating that it was quite large. But you saw the fish and you know it was smaller than he is suggesting. You want to tell the story right, so you correct your husband in public.

Like most men, your husband is offended and embarrassed at being corrected in front of your friends. When you go home that night, what could have been a romantic night together turns into a fight. He's angry, and now he's not speaking to you.

Stop and Consider First — Before You Speak

Now let's look at that situation from the perspective of a woman who *considers* before she acts. It's the same scenario — you're with your dear friends and having a wonderful time, when your husband starts telling the fish story. Instead of immediately speaking, you *consider* and *examine* the situation first. You think to yourself, *I don't think that's exactly the way that it was, but is this fish story really that important? No. Will correcting him bring about excellence in our relationship? No. Is it worthwhile saying something that will embarrass or offend him? Again, no. So I am not going to open my mouth, and I am certainly not going to embarrass my husband in public.*

Your husband tells his story without your correction. You return home and have a nice, romantic time together, and you wake up the next morning refreshed. Do you see the difference between the woman who *considered* her actions and the woman who did not consider her actions?

Consider This: Ask Questions *Before* You Act

God has given us something very powerful — He's given us a beautiful mind, so we can stop and consider and ask ourselves, *Should I do this, or should I do that? Are my actions going to be excellent? Is it vital that I do this? Is it worthwhile for me to do that?* These are very important questions we should ask ourselves before we decide what we will do or say.

This is what the wise woman in Proverbs 31:16 did; she looked at that field, and she asked questions *before* she bought it. She may have asked, "Is this field *worth* my time looking at it? Is it *excellent*? Is it going to bring *good* to my family?" This is the example we must follow as wise women and wise men in relationships. We must *consider* — and then let wisdom direct our actions and words.

In her program, Denise candidly shared that she has done both — considered the situation before acting or speaking but also acting or speaking without any consideration — and she has learned from both scenarios. She confessed that she is much better now at pausing to consider and examine a situation than she was many years ago when she was first learning these principles. She has reaped the good fruit from considering what is excellent, vital, and worthwhile. And you can too!

Consider This: The Word of God Is Your Medicine

As we're making decisions about what to say and do, it's very important that we consider the Word of God and how powerful it is. You may say, or you may have heard others say, "I don't read my Bible that much. I try to, but I'm a really busy person and I don't have time to read God's Word." Proverbs 4:20-22 says, "My son, give attention to my words; incline your ear to my sayings. Do not let them depart from your eyes; keep them in the midst of your heart; for they are life to those who find them, and health to all their flesh." It is powerful to read the Word of God and keep it in our heart, and when we do, it is life and health to us.

Consider this: If you're struggling with sickness, is it worth scrolling on your phone for hours looking at random things? That activity is not excellent, it's not vital, and it's not worth your time. It's actually *stealing* your time and keeping you from using your eyes and your mind to put the Word of God in your heart, which *will* change your health. In her program, Denise shared an example of the power of God's healing Word.

> There was a man who was living in a climate that was very hot and humid, and he got a horrible disease on his skin. The doctor's treatments were not helping him. They tried putting medicine on it, but he was in misery. He couldn't sleep because his skin was itching and burning all the time.
>
> Then somebody asked him, "Do you know that the Word of God is medicine to your flesh, and if you read the Bible, it will be healing to your body?" So the man decided to take the Word of God just like you take medicine — after breakfast, after lunch, and before bedtime. Three times a day, he put the Scriptures into his eyes, into his heart, and into his mouth. And after a few weeks, the disease — that had made him miserable, and no doctor could cure — completely left his body. It was the Word of God that brought healing to his flesh and body.

Consider This: How Much Mercy Are You Giving Others?

Proverbs 3:3 and 4 says, "Let not mercy and truth forsake you; bind them around your neck, write them on the tablet of your heart, and so find favor and high esteem in the sight of God and man." What a promise! Who among us does not want to find favor and high esteem in the sight of God and man? We *all* want that!

But to receive this promise from the Lord, we first need to do what this verse instructs: "Let not mercy and truth forsake [us]." We need to consider how much mercy we're extending to others and how much truth we are taking in. We must *consider* these instructions and then *decide* what to do. Will we give mercy? Will we hold truth in our heart? Or will we judge people and hold unforgiveness toward them?

Ask yourself, "How important is it that I forgive and show mercy?" Proverbs 3:3 and 4 contains the answer: If you want to find and receive favor and high esteem in the sight of God and man, it's very important. It's so important that the Word instructs us to write this verse on the tablet of our heart and bind it around our neck. In other words, don't let mercy and truth get away from you. Let them be ingrained in your heart and the first thing that comes from your lips.

Consider This: How Much of the Word of God Are You Taking In Daily?

It's very important that we develop a taste for the Word of God and understand that it brings health to our body. In her program, Denise shared another example of the power of God's Word.

> I once knew a woman who had a really hard job. She would start early in the morning, work hard all day, and work until midnight every day. When she first started that job, she found out she had cancer in her pancreas, but she needed the job because she was financially supporting her family who lived in another country.
>
> She found out that the Word of God had healing promises in it. Despite her long hours and busy work schedule, she read the entire Bible in two months! That took time and commitment, but she considered the importance of the Word of God. After

two months of spending all that time in the Word, the pancreatic cancer was gone from her body — she was completely healed!

It is worth considering that you may need to spend more time reading or listening to God's Word. There's health for you in the Bible. There's His promise that as you extend or give more mercy to others and hold on to His truth, you're going to receive mercy back, and you're going to find favor and high esteem in the sight of God and man.

God's Word carries so much wisdom and power for your life. As you work through these lessons, hear what His Word is saying to you. Remember the power of considering before you act and speak. Ask these questions: *Is this vital? Is this excellent? Is this worth my time?* Consider these things and make changes so that you will reap good fruit in your life.

STUDY QUESTIONS

Be diligent to present yourself approved to God, a worker who does not need to be ashamed, rightly dividing the word of truth.
— 2 Timothy 2:15

1. *Consider* the healing power in the Word of God when you read Proverbs 4:20-22; Psalm 107:20; Isaiah 53:4 and 5; and First Peter 2:24.
2. Proverbs 3:3,4 says, "Let not mercy and truth forsake you; bind them around your neck, write them on the tablet of your heart, and so find favor and high esteem in the sight of God and man." *Consider* how much mercy you are giving to others. What is the result of sowing mercy when others need it? (*See* Galatians 6:7.)
3. Denise shared that the Word of God carries wisdom and power for your life. How hungry are you for God's Word? Read Psalm 119 aloud and savor the fellowship with the Lord as you draw near to Him through His Word.

PRACTICAL APPLICATION

But be doers of the word, and not hearers only, deceiving yourselves.
— James 1:22

1. Proverbs 31:16 instructs, "She considers a field and buys it; from her profits she plants a vineyard." This godly woman *considered* what she

did before she did it. And likewise, we can consider our actions and our decisions every day. What decisions do you have right in front of you that you need to take some time to consider and think deeply about before deciding what to do? Take some time to look at those decisions carefully before acting on them. Ask the Lord for His counsel before you take a step.

2. We must *consider* how our words will impact others before we open our mouth and speak. Ask yourself, *If I say this or do this, is it really that important? Is it excellent? Is it worth my while? How much better would it be if I kept my mouth closed?* Words are creative or destructive; they create or destroy. Think about the words you have spoken in the last few days. Did they build up others? Were they encouraging? Notice what the Word of God admonishes: "Let no foul or polluting language, nor evil word nor unwholesome or worthless talk [ever] come out of your mouth, but only such [speech] as is good and beneficial to the spiritual progress of others, as is fitting to the need and the occasion, that it may be a blessing and give grace (God's favor) to those who hear it" (Ephesians 4:29 *AMPC*). Take a few minutes to write out what this scripture means in your own words. How can you be a "doer" of this passage?

LESSON 6

TOPIC
There Is a Big Giver Inside You

SCRIPTURES
1. **Proverbs 31:20** — She extends her hand to the poor, yes, she reaches out her hands to the needy.
2. **John 3:16** — For God so loved the world that He gave His only begotten Son, that whoever believes in Him should not perish but have everlasting life.
3. **Matthew 11:28,29** — Come to Me, all you who labor and are heavy laden, and I will give you rest. Take My yoke upon you and learn from Me, for I am gentle and lowly in heart, and you will find rest for your souls.

4. **Hebrews 4:15,16** — For we do not have a High Priest who cannot sympathize with our weaknesses, but was in all points tempted as we are, yet without sin. Let us therefore come boldly to the throne of grace, that we may obtain mercy and find grace to help in time of need.
5. **Matthew 6:34** — Therefore do not worry about tomorrow, for tomorrow will worry about its own things. Sufficient for the day is its own trouble.
6. **Ephesians 3:20,21** — Now to Him who is able to do exceedingly abundantly above all that we ask or think, according to the power that works in us, to Him be glory in the church by Christ Jesus to all generations, forever and ever. Amen.

SYNOPSIS

Proverbs 31 teaches that we are to be generous givers who help those in need. Our model is God Himself, who is the greatest giver of all; He sent Jesus, His only begotten Son, to redeem us on the Cross. The source of His giving is His great love for the whole world. He saw our need, and God did exceedingly, abundantly above all we could imagine to meet this need. We are to follow His example by giving to our families and those in need. We can give anything we have — our time, prayers, encouragement, and anything else that the Holy Spirit leads us to give. And because we can never out-give God, we can give boldly and faithfully without fear of lack.

The emphasis of this lesson:

Through His Word and the Holy Spirit who lives within us, God speaks to us about giving to others. We can *choose* to be a giver every single day by ministering to the needy, praying for them, offering what we have, and sharing our love. When we give freely, lives are changed.

There are incredible treasures we can receive from the study of Proverbs 31. Remember, many scholars believe that it was Bathsheba whom the Holy Spirit used to pen these writings. Though Bathsheba had been a participant in sin, she and King David repented. And God forgave her — and David! God lifted her to a place of confidence so she could instruct her son on how to be a great king and share the traits he should look for in a virtuous wife.

And thousands of years later, we still have these wise instructions to guide our path.

As you study Proverbs 31, expect God to speak to your heart through the wisdom and instruction of these scriptures. He communicates to you through His Word — the Bible. His Word is supernatural! And when you read the Bible and take it in, God works through His Word to help you make adjustments in your life. The previous lesson touched on taking His Word like medicine — prioritizing reading, speaking, and listening to God's Word. When we do that, it has the power to bring healing to our body. That's how powerful the Word is!

The Virtuous Woman Is a Giver

In Proverbs 31:20, as Bathsheba instructed her son Solomon on the kind of wife he should choose, she shared a key attribute of a godly wife: "She extends her hand to the poor, yes, she reaches out her hands to the needy." In this amazing verse, Bathsheba was advising her son to find a woman who is a giver, not someone who is all about herself. She told him to choose someone who is not thinking, "What about me? Poor me!" but is thinking instead, "How can I give to somebody else?" What a wise and powerful piece of instruction!

We have the greatest example of a giver in our God! John 3:16 says, "For God so loved the world that *He gave* His only begotten Son, that whoever believes in Him should not perish but have everlasting life." That is what love does — it gives! Bathsheba was saying to Solomon, in essence, "Find a woman who has love in her heart, not just for herself but for others. Find someone who *wants* to give."

Notice that John 3:16 says, "For God so loved *the world*...." It's not just us, our neighbors, and our friends and family that He loves. God also loves those who will never love Him in return. He loves the whole world — even those who will never call out His name. He loves them so much that He gave His only begotten Son and the offer of everlasting life. That's our loving God. He IS love! And He gives generously and abundantly!

The Power of Giving Changes Lives

One of the ways we can express love is by giving. In fact, love is *the source* of our giving. In her program, Denise recounted her experience of ministering for many years at a drug and alcohol hospital in Moscow. She and her team made monthly visits to a section of the hospital that housed approximately 100 women. They would bring the women Bibles and gifts, such as candy and small books, as well as love, care, and hugs. Denise shared:

> The women would watch us suspiciously as we set up the gifts, books, and flowers on a decorated table in the middle of the hallway. At first, the women were standoffish and cautious. They would say things like, "What could you have to say to me? My life is so terrible. I don't know how you could have any help for me."
>
> Many of these women were in great pain because of the drugs or alcohol. Many of the young mothers had lost their children, while older mothers had lost their whole family. As a result, these women had reason to feel rejected; they had reason to feel like they were a failure.
>
> But the love of God came to them through us. As we gave our gifts and poured out our love to them, we watched as the love of God absolutely changed the countenance of these women. We told them about Jesus, sang songs to them, and gave them Bibles. Some of them were crying and letting us pray with them. And when it was time for us to go, they hugged us, thanked us for coming, and told us to come back.

That's the power of giving! And it's the picture of what Bathsheba shared in Proverbs 31:20: "She extends her hand to the poor, yes, she reaches out her hands to the needy." Bathsheba was saying to her son, Solomon, "Choose a woman who *wants* to give, who doesn't hold her fist tight, refusing to share but instead lives with open hands and an open heart, reaching out to people who are in need."

Choose To Give From a Heart of Love

Giving is an attitude, and we can have this attitude every day of our life. Every day, each one of us is given 24 hours. And in those 24 hours, we can *choose* to be a giver.

You can *choose* to be a giver to your family. Give your family compliments, encouragement, hugs, attention, a listening ear, and forgiveness. Tell your children they are awesome and encourage them by telling them you believe in them and that they are going to have a great day at school. Pray with them. Let your husband know that you are standing in faith with him. Thank your husband for all his hard work. Let him know you appreciate him and show him affection.

You can actively do your very best to be a giver all day. Remind yourself that the day ahead of you is not just an opportunity to feel sorry for yourself. Instead, you can *choose* to give. You can have the attitude that your 24 hours is an opportunity — and your responsibility — to impart something to somebody else. That's powerful!

Remember — it is a privilege to be able to give whatever you have to offer. Whether you are sharing money, a smile, clothes, time, grace, forgiveness, or anything else you may have, being able to give is a blessing. And your giving is truly coming from a single source — the love in your heart.

Giving Is More Blessed Than Receiving

Jesus said it is more blessed to give than to receive (*see* Acts 20:35). Have you ever noticed that? Denise shared in her program, "I know that when we would minister at the drug and alcohol hospital, we all felt a lot better after we came out of that place than we did before we went in. Why? Because we had given, and it's more blessed to give than it is to receive."

We see this freedom to give in Jesus. He was God in the flesh, and He could have done anything — and *He chose to give.* Jesus said, "Come to Me, all you who labor and are heavy laden, and I will give you rest. Take My yoke upon you and learn from Me, for I am gentle and lowly in heart, and you will find rest for your souls" (Matthew 11:28,29). Jesus had — and still has — an attitude of giving. Jesus is inviting you to come to Him because He wants to give you rest for your soul — your mind, your will, and your emotions. Isn't that powerful? Jesus is a giver.

God the Father is such a giver that He gave Jesus to the whole world. He even invites us to enter into His presence in His throne room through the blood that Jesus shed for us on the Cross. Hebrews 4:15 says, "For we do not have a High Priest who cannot sympathize with our weaknesses, but was in all points tempted as we are, yet without sin." When Jesus came to earth, He left the glory of Heaven. Fully man, He was tempted in every way, just like we are. Even though He was tempted, He didn't sin. Yet He has compassion for us.

Hebrews 4:16 goes on to say, "Let us therefore come boldly to the throne of grace, that we may obtain mercy and find grace to help in time of need."

Again, we see that God wants to give us something! He's inviting us to His throne of grace. He wants us to come into His presence and *receive* — to obtain mercy and find grace in our time of need.

Extend Your Hands To Give to Others in Need

When we give so others can receive, that's when we're the most like Jesus. In her program, Denise recalled that the drug and alcohol hospital in Moscow, where she and her team would minister to the ladies, was not a pretty place. She said, "I remember thinking, *I feel more like Jesus giving to these women than I do just reading my Bible.*" She went on to say that she felt that way because she was being like Jesus! Why? Because she was giving of herself — despite the circumstances that surrounded her. Likewise, when you give, *you are being like Jesus.*

The wisdom found in Proverbs 31:20 is a model for godly women and wives, but it also extends to men and husbands as well. We should see ourselves as givers whose hands are open and extended to impart to the poor and those in need. On the program, Denise shared an inspirational story that she had recently heard on the news about people who gave generously.

> There was a couple with five children, all of whom had been adopted. Sadly, their neighbor, a single mother with three children, was dying of cancer, and the children would have no place to go after she died. So the family with five children adopted the neighbor's three children.
>
> When word got out about this family's generosity, the whole city came together to buy the family a new house. They even gave them extra money and groceries. This family didn't choose to adopt the three orphaned children expecting to get something in return. All they wanted to do was to give these three children a safe home and family — to be a blessing. And in return, *they* were blessed!

Obey the Giver on the Inside — the Holy Spirit

The Bible says when we receive Jesus as our Lord and Savior that the Holy Spirit is "given us…in our hearts" (*see* 2 Corinthians 1:22). The Holy Spirit is a gift to us from God, and He lovingly and intentionally places the Holy Spirit inside us to seal us unto Himself. The Holy Spirit is a giver, and the Holy Spirit is a lover. He dwells within us, and He wants to lead us in our giving to others.

If you are sensitive to His leading and listen for His voice, the Holy Spirit will speak to you and tell you how you can give to and love others. He may tell you when to give someone a hug and an encouraging word that he or she is going to make it. He'll show you how to reach out to others and pray for them, give them a gift, or tell them that you care about them, and that God loves them. The Holy Spirit encourages you to do these things because He's a giver! He's the Giver inside you, reminding you that it is your opportunity and privilege to give.

Matthew 6:34 tells us, "Therefore do not worry about tomorrow, for tomorrow will worry about its own things. Sufficient for the day is its own trouble." You may be wondering, *How can I give like this? How can I interrupt my busy schedule to call someone and pray for them? I can barely take care of my family, my job, and my house as it is right now.*

Here's the good news — you only have to think about *today*. Matthew 6:34 is saying to not even think about tomorrow, because tomorrow will take care of itself. If you hear the Holy Spirit speaking to you *today* to give — whether it's a hug, a word of encouragement, a phone call, a visit to somebody, or something else He's leading you to do — then do it! Do it quickly. Do it when He tells you to do it because then you'll be *in agreement with the Holy Spirit*. You're saying, "Holy Spirit, I hear You, and I'm going to do what you need me to do right now."

When you recognize His leading and you quickly follow His direction, you'll get into the flow of being a giver, and you will begin to understand how great it is to give. You'll see that it truly is greater to *give* than it is to receive.

Seeing Lives Changed Through Your Giving

The greatest thing about giving when the Holy Spirit directs you to do so is that you're being obedient to the Lord. But sometimes when you give, you get the added blessing of *seeing* that person blessed. You get to see their life changed and can rejoice with them, which will give you great pleasure. It is important to Jesus that you give! As you obey the Holy Spirit and give what and when He asks you to give, you will learn what a giver He is!

Maybe you're already giving, but He may desire for you to give more. Or maybe you need to offer forgiveness. When you give forgiveness, you are in agreement with the Holy Spirit! Remember — you can *never* out-give God. Ephesians 3:20 says that our God is "able to do exceedingly abundantly above all that we ask or think, according to the power that works in us." That's what *God* wants to give — *exceedingly, abundantly above all we can ask or think.*

But God wants *us* to give. Know that you can never, ever outgive Him. He will always give back to you more than you gave. It is so encouraging to listen to the Holy Spirit as He directs you on how and what to give. By obeying Him, you are giving the love of God, and it's touching others and changing their life. And you become a source where God's love can flow out to others!

STUDY QUESTIONS

> Be diligent to present yourself approved to God, a worker
> who does not need to be ashamed, rightly dividing the word of truth.
> — 2 Timothy 2:15

1. Second Corinthians 9:6 (*AMPC*) says, "[Remember] this: he who sows sparingly and grudgingly will also reap sparingly and grudgingly, and he who sows generously [that blessings may come to someone] will also reap generously and with blessings." What type of attitude is God looking for in *us* when we give?
2. Second Corinthians 9:7 (*AMPC*) continues, "Let each one [give] as he has made up his own mind and purposed in his heart, not reluctantly or sorrowfully or under compulsion, for God loves (He takes pleasure in, prizes above other things, and is unwilling to abandon or to do without) a cheerful (joyous, "prompt to do it") giver [whose heart is in his giving]." What is *God's* attitude toward a cheerful giver?
3. Second Corinthians 9:8 (*AMPC*) admonishes, "And God is able to make all grace (every favor and earthly blessing) come to you in abundance, so that you may always and under all circumstances and whatever the need be self-sufficient [possessing enough to require no aid or support and furnished in abundance for every good work and charitable donation]." What does God's Word promise us as we give?

PRACTICAL APPLICATION

> But be doers of the word,
> and not hearers only, deceiving yourselves.
> —James 1:22

1. Finances aren't the only thing you can give to others. You can give of your time, your talent, and your strength. Take inventory of what you have to give to others and mobilize your giving by acting on the promptings of the Holy Spirit. Write a list of the things you can give to others and pray over it. With a willing heart, ask God to use you in the area of giving.

2. "Give, and it will be given to you: good measure, pressed down, shaken together, and running over will be put into your bosom. For with the same measure that you use, it will be measured back to you" (Luke 6:38). What does this verse promise will happen when you give to others? If you've been slow to obey God in the past in the area of giving, ask Him to forgive you, and purpose in your heart to obey Him — beginning today!

LESSON 7

TOPIC

Your New Clothes — Strength and Honor

SCRIPTURES

1. **Proverbs 31:25** — Strength and honor are her clothing; she shall rejoice in time to come.

2. **Psalm 45:13-15** — The royal daughter is all glorious within the palace; her clothing is woven with gold. She shall be brought to the King in robes of many colors; the virgins, her companions who follow her, shall be brought to You. With gladness and rejoicing they shall be brought; they shall enter the King's palace.

3. **Isaiah 61:10** — I will greatly rejoice in the Lord, my soul shall be joyful in my God; for He has clothed me with the garments of salvation,

He has covered me with the robe of righteousness, as a bridegroom decks himself with ornaments, and as a bride adorns herself with her jewels.

4. **2 Corinthians 4:7** — But we have this treasure in earthen vessels, that the excellence of the power may be of God and not of us.
5. **Philippians 1:3,4** — I thank my God upon every remembrance of you, always in every prayer of mine making request for you all with joy.
6. **Philippians 1:18** — What then? Only that in every way, whether in pretense or in truth, Christ is preached; and in this I rejoice, yes, and will rejoice.
7. **Philippians 2:2** — Fulfill my joy by being like-minded, having the same love, being of one accord, of one mind.
8. **Philippians 2:17** — Yes, and if I am being poured out as a drink offering on the sacrifice and service of your faith, I am glad and rejoice with you all.
9. **Philippians 4:4** — Rejoice in the Lord always. Again I will say, rejoice!

SYNOPSIS

Another aspect of the character of a Proverbs 31 woman is that she is clothed with strength and honor. We are adorned with strength and honor because the Holy Spirit lives within us. This is how God sees us, and as we learn to recognize this amazing treasure He has put inside us, we become empowered through Him to overcome difficult situations. He gives us the strength and ability to rejoice at all times.

The emphasis of this lesson:

We are clothed in strength and honor because of the One who lives within us. The real you is *not* the clothes you wear on the outside but the majestic and magnificent glory that you have on the inside as a born-again Christian. You have been forgiven and redeemed by God. And through His strength, you can rejoice — no matter what you are facing!

Learn From the Wisdom Contained in God's Word

When Jesus went to the Cross, He took on Himself not only our sin but also the pain and rejection we've experienced throughout our lives. He has freed us from our past, and He brings healing to our heart. The power that comes from His forgiveness is amazing, and when His forgiveness comes into our lives, no matter what we've done, He can lift us up to a place of freedom and confidence in Him.

That's what God did for Bathsheba — the author of Proverbs 31. How could God take such an imperfect woman — one who committed adultery, was an accomplice to a murder, and who lied and deceived — and raise her to the place of a teacher who could instruct her son on how to be a godly man and king? How could He transform her into someone who could teach women through the ages how to be virtuous women? This glorious transformation was made possible through forgiveness — *the great and miraculous and marvelous power of forgiveness that we receive through Jesus*!

Proverbs 31 contains exciting and powerful lessons for our lives. Like Proverbs 31:16, which tells us to *consider* first — to *think* about it — before we act. We are to consider His Word and His direction through the Holy Spirit as we make decisions. We don't just do things because we feel like doing them. We can *choose* what we will do, considering first how our words or actions will affect other people or even ourselves. No matter how we may feel, we can put a smile on our face, say "This is the day the Lord has made," and be a blessing to people.

Through Bathsheba's (and King David's) story, we see how God can take a bad situation and bring good from it. We also discovered that we can never outgive God, and He can turn our situation around. And because of His love and forgiveness and the power of the Holy Spirit, we can become givers who bring honor and glory to God. That's the power of transformation and redemption that Bathsheba experienced and wrote about.

The Lord Sees You — The *Real* You

Another trait of a virtuous woman is learning how to give, even out of her pain. Proverbs 31:25 says, "Strength and honor are her clothing; she shall rejoice in time to come." You might wonder, *What does "strength and honor are her clothing" mean?*

The answer to this question is found in the verses preceding Proverbs 31:25. This chapter of scripture describes how we are called to do difficult things — such as staying the course, not giving up, praying in the night, getting up early, and using our gifts and talents. We are to do these things, push through hard times, and present something excellent. And the result of all our effort, obedience, and faithfulness is this: "Strength and honor are her clothing; she shall rejoice in time to come."

Think about how amazing this is! The Lord sees what every one of us goes through — including *you*! He sees the difficulties. He sees the hardships. And when you push through the difficult seasons and circumstances and do the right thing, it *clothes* you. You may have on a T-shirt right now or your pajamas or an old jacket — but God sees something different. He sees something on the *inside* of you that's magnificent. He sees strength and honor in you.

Clothed on the Inside With Glory

Have you ever considered how the Bible describes the person who has pushed through, did not give up, but rather did the hard thing? Maybe you love somebody who is very difficult to live with and you have to forgive often, be patient often, serve often, and believe the best of this person over and over again. But you keep pushing through.

Maybe your outward clothes don't look magnificent but consider what is happening *inside* you. Inwardly, you are dressed in strength and honor. You are clothed in beauty, comeliness, excellency, glory, honor, and majesty. This is what you look like in the spirit! It is the truth about who you are as you live in harmony and obedience with God's Word. When you go through difficult things and you don't give up but instead push forward and do your very best with the help of the Holy Spirit, this is what you look like. It's the *real* you!

Psalm 45:13-15 says, "The *royal daughter* **is all glorious within the palace; her clothing** is woven with gold. She shall be brought to the King in robes of many colors; the virgins, her companions who follow her, shall be brought to You. With gladness and rejoicing they shall be brought; they shall enter the King's palace." Friend, the blood of Jesus makes *you* a royal daughter. Even though life can be very hard, know that the difficult circumstances and events you encounter don't take *from* you. When you push through the hard situations, your faithful persistence *brings* beautiful clothing into your heart and character. And being dressed as a royal daughter is powerful!

Isaiah 61:10 says, "I will greatly rejoice in the Lord, my soul shall be joyful in my God; for He has clothed me with the garments of salvation, He has covered me with the robe of righteousness, as a bridegroom decks himself with ornaments, and as a bride adorns herself with her jewels." This verse shows you what you truly look like — not what you're wearing on the outside, but what you're clothed with on the inside. You are beautiful, and you are powerful!

Know the Treasure That Is Inside You

To realize the truth about the garments God has inwardly clothed us with, the Bible says we're to be still and know that He is God (*see* Psalm 46:10). There is so much busyness going on around us, and we're so busy ourselves. We're doing everything we know how to do; we're taking care of so many things in our lives, we're showing love and forgiveness to others, and in the midst of that, we're planning — always planning. *We are so busy!*

But the Bible calls us to pause, be still, and get quiet. Why? So we can come to know and recognize this *glory* and *majesty* that is inside us. Second Corinthians 4:7 says, "…We have this treasure in earthen vessels, that the excellence of the power may be of God and not of us." We have a *treasure on the inside*. You are so glorious on the inside — more glorious than the most fabulous cathedral, and more majestic than a palace decked with gold. So you have jewels, pearls, and gold adorning the inside of you, so to speak.

The fact that this glorious, heavenly treasure is placed in earthen vessels is amazing. The glory of God is *inside you*. As you push through difficult circumstances and "do the hard thing," what you're doing enhances that glory. And that glory inside you increases as you are pushing through. You can declare, "God, this is difficult, but You've given me Your power. I have this treasure on the inside, and I'm pushing through all these difficult things. And I receive these wonderful clothes of strength and honor that You're putting on me."

There Is Power in Knowing Who Lives Inside You

There are times when we don't want to be quiet. It's not always easy to be still. To emphasize this point, Denise shared a personal example in her program. She said, "I remember when I was a little girl, and my mom would make clothes for me. I would have to try on the dress so she could hem it, but I would fidget and move around. And mom would say, 'Denise, would you please be still?'"

That's what the Holy Spirit is saying. He is asking you to be quiet for a few minutes so you may know that He is God and living inside you. Be still and recognize that you have a treasure inside you — you don't have to busy yourself every single moment of every single day. You can be *quiet*, and you can *recognize* that He is God. You can know that He put a treasure inside you, and He is clothing you with majesty, excellence, honor, and beauty.

In Christ, we are royal daughters. This is the reality for us! We may not see it with our physical eyes, but we can see it with the eyes of our heart. When we understand who really lives in us, it gives us power. And it is for this reason that God is directing us to quiet ourselves, take time with Him, and *recognize* that He dwells within us and has placed strength and honor inside us.

Rejoice Through the One Who Lives Inside You

Proverbs 31:25 continues, "…She shall rejoice in time to come." Your ability to rejoice comes from the treasure that's inside you. As we recognize that treasure, we can rejoice. The book of Philippians was written by the apostle Paul while he was in a horrible prison. Yet in his difficult situation, he found many ways to rejoice.

In Philippians 1:3 and 4, Paul said, "I thank my God upon every remembrance of you, always in every prayer of mine making request for you all with joy." One of the ways Paul rejoiced was by praying for other people, and he prayed *with joy*. When we pray for somebody, we are not to pray for them with sadness but with joy. It's a *privilege* for Christians to pray for somebody — and we can be joyful about that.

Paul went on to say, "What then? Only that in every way, whether in pretense or in truth, Christ is preached; and in this I rejoice, yes, and will rejoice" (Philippians 1:18). The apostle Paul was *choosing* to rejoice. Even though he knew that some people were preaching the Gospel for the wrong reasons (*see* Philippians 1:15-17), the Gospel was still being preached. He was suffering in a horrible prison, but he reminded himself that "whether in pretense or in truth, Christ is preached." No matter what others were doing, if the Gospel was being preached, he said, in essence, "I'm going to rejoice about it. I'm even going to rejoice again."

Oftentimes we may witness something being done for the wrong motives but good can still come from it, so we can still rejoice. How can we rejoice when we feel like there's injustice? We can do it because of the treasure that's inside us. We're clothed on the inside with majesty, excellence, strength, and honor. And from that place, we can say, "I'm going to rejoice, and I'm going to rejoice again."

There Is Power in Rejoicing

In Philippians 2:2, the apostle Paul again rejoiced, saying, "Fulfill my joy by being like-minded, having the same love, being of one accord, of one mind." Paul was joyful that people were like-minded in the Lord. If you have people around you, and you're all believing or thinking the same way, that's a reason to rejoice. If somebody's in agreement with you and stands with you, you can rejoice about that. Joy is powerful!

But what if agreement is in short supply? Philippians 2:17 says, "Yes, and if I am being poured out as a drink offering on the sacrifice and service of your faith, I am glad and rejoice with you all." Like the apostle Paul, you may feel like you're being poured out. You may be a single mom, or you have a demanding job, and you're also taking care of your family or your house or a sick child. Your life is not your own, and your life is being poured out for others. The apostle Paul said, "I *rejoice* that my life is being poured out." That's a powerful revelation!

When life gets hard, we tend to wonder how we're going to make it. We may tell ourselves, "I can't do this. This is too much." Sometimes we enter into self-pity, but that just takes the strength and joy right out of us. But what if we recognize the treasure inside us — that excellency, that honor, that strength — and we choose to say, "I know my life is not my own. I'm being poured out, but I'm going to rejoice?" Do you know what that does? It gives you more strength! Hallelujah!

Gain Strength by Rejoicing Always

The apostle Paul wrote about another opportunity to rejoice in Philippians 4. Paul heard about a situation that arose between two sisters who were once co-laborers with him in the Gospel. But now they were in conflict with one another, and he heard about it and told them to make the situation right. In Philippians 4:4, he said about that situation, "Rejoice in the Lord always. Again I will say, rejoice!" He said to the women, in essence, "Don't get sad about this situation. Don't get upset. Rejoice! And again I say, rejoice!"

When considering your own life, you may be saying, "These are not things to rejoice about. I don't *want* to rejoice." But remember, if you rejoice from the place of knowing the treasure inside you, it gives you strength! It gives you power! When you choose to rejoice always, as Philippians instructs, you are recognizing the One who is inside you who gives you the strength and power to rejoice.

The One inside you — the Holy Spirit — is not caught off guard or upset about the things that are going on today. It's through Him that you have strength within you to deal with everything you're facing. And that strength is clothing you so you can rejoice always — even when things are difficult. This is the Proverbs 31 woman — one who is not knocked down by life but instead is clothed in strength, honor, excellency, and majesty, which gives her joy in every season. And that's *you*!

STUDY QUESTIONS

> Be diligent to present yourself approved to God, a worker
> who does not need to be ashamed, rightly dividing the word of truth.
> — 2 Timothy 2:15

1. If you are facing difficult circumstances, it's important you know where they originated. According to John 10:10, if something is trying to steal, kill, or destroy you, where/who did it come from? Realize God is with you, and He sent Jesus to pay the price so you can live victoriously over everything that has come against your life: sickness, sin, and lack. (*Read* First John 4:4; First Peter 2:24; Isaiah 53:5; and Third John 2.)
2. Denise talked about the blessing of being in one accord and of one mind. What does Psalm 133:1 say about dwelling together in unity? Is that something to rejoice about? (*See* Philippians 2:2.) Notice what happened in Acts 2:46 and 47 when the Early Church continued "daily with one accord in the temple." What was the result of their unity as described in Acts 2:47?
3. According to God's Word, where does your strength come from? (*Consider* Psalm 18:32; Psalm 27:1; Psalm 29:11; Psalm 71:16; Psalm 84:7; Philippians 4:13; Ephesians 6:10; and Nehemiah 8:10.)

PRACTICAL APPLICATION

> But be doers of the word,
> and not hearers only, deceiving yourselves.
> —James 1:22

1. Sometimes life can be so hard that you have to look around and say, "I'm looking for something to rejoice about." Take a moment and write down five things you are thankful for. Now, from your heart, rejoice about and thank God for those things. How did this moment of rejoicing and thankfulness impact your attitude? Make a habit of giving thanks and rejoicing every day when you wake up and every night when you go to bed.

2. In this lesson, Denise taught about what you are clothed with on the inside. Using the Word of God as your mirror, describe your royal wardrobe.

3. Take time to acknowledge the presence of God within you. Yield to His presence to overcome life's difficulties. Worship the Lord from your heart for a few minutes, and then pray this prayer: *Father, I just thank You so much for that treasure that's inside me that gives me the ability to push through any kind of difficult situation. Your presence within me does not have to bow to circumstances and the problems of this life. But Your presence in me, Your strength in me is greater than anything that is in this world. By the Power of the Holy Spirit, I take hold of and recognize that power as my very own. In Jesus' name. Amen.*

LESSON 8

TOPIC

'Who's in Control — Me or My Mouth?'

SCRIPTURES

1. **Proverbs 31:26** — She opens her mouth with wisdom, and on her tongue is the law of kindness.

2. **Proverbs 18:21** — Death and life are in the power of the tongue, and those who love it will eat its fruit.
3. **Proverbs 21:23** — Whoever guards his mouth and tongue keeps his soul from troubles.
4. **Proverbs 18:8** — The words of a talebearer are like tasty trifles, and they go down into the inmost body.
5. **Proverbs 18:20** — A man's stomach shall be satisfied from the fruit of his mouth; from the produce of his lips he shall be filled.
6. **Proverbs 15:28** — The heart of the righteous studies how to answer, but the mouth of the wicked pours forth evil.
7. **Proverbs 16:23,24** — The heart of the wise teaches his mouth, and adds learning to his lips. Pleasant words are like a honeycomb, sweetness to the soul and health to the bones.
8. **Proverbs 15:1,2** — A soft answer turns away wrath, but a harsh word stirs up anger. The tongue of the wise uses knowledge rightly, but the mouth of fools pours forth foolishness.
9. **Proverbs 12:14** — A man will be satisfied with good by the fruit of his mouth, and the recompense of a man's hands will be rendered to him.
10. **Proverbs 12:18** — There is one who speaks like the piercings of a sword, but the tongue of the wise promotes health.
11. **Ephesians 4:32** — And be kind to one another, tenderhearted, forgiving one another, even as God in Christ forgave you.

SYNOPSIS

Proverbs 31:26 tells us that a virtuous woman "opens her mouth with wisdom, and on her tongue is the law of kindness." This principle is essential to positive, godly interactions with others, especially your husband. Your words make their way into your inner being, affecting your physical and emotional wellness as well as your relationships. Through your righteousness in Christ, you have the Holy Spirit within you, and He is well able to help you to speak wise, grace-filled words that bring blessings to those around you.

The emphasis of this lesson:

By leaning on the Holy Spirit, you can learn to guard your mouth and carefully consider your words *before* you speak. As you commit to

responding to your husband with wisdom and grace, you can enjoy more peaceful, fruitful times in your marriage and avoid unnecessary troubles.

Proverbs 31:26 says, "She opens her mouth with wisdom, and on her tongue is the law of kindness." Oh, what excellent instruction that is! One of the most important areas of your whole body is your tongue. The Bible says in Proverbs 18:21, "Death and life are in the power of the tongue, and those who love it will eat its fruit." The words we choose to speak are so powerful that they can bring life or death!

Guard Your Tongue To Keep Your Soul From Trouble

The instruction Bathsheba gave in Proverbs 31:26 is vital to the quality of your life and the quality of other people's lives too. And Proverbs 21:23 concurs. It says, "Whoever guards his mouth and tongue keeps his soul from troubles." Do you want to keep your soul from troubles? Of course, you do! We all want to keep our mind, will, and emotions from being distressed, but there is something we have to do first — we must guard our mouth and our tongue. In other words, we must be mindful of the words we allow to exit our mouth.

The lesson of guarding your tongue is very important in marriage. After Adam and Eve fell, a curse came upon the earth. Genesis 3:16 explains the portion that fell to Eve and to all women — a desire to control her husband. By human nature (the flesh), women are very tempted to use their mouth to control, criticize, complain, or "teach" their husband. But the mouth is very powerful for creating life *or* death (*see* Proverbs 18:21), so we must guard it.

In her program, Denise shared that when she teaches women on the topic of guarding their tongue, she encourages the women to guard what they say to their husbands. And when Denise asks them, "How was your week?" "How did it go?" or "What kind of decisions did you make through the week?" many of the women say, "I didn't criticize my husband" "I didn't complain" "I didn't try to teach him" or "I didn't try to correct him." And their response is often followed by this: "And do you know what? It was one of the most peaceful weeks of my life." Why is peace the result? It's because these women were able to control their tongues by applying the wisdom of the Word of God.

What Words Are We Feeding Ourselves?

Now let's look at Proverbs 18:8, which says, "The words of a talebearer are like tasty trifles, and they go down into the inmost body." Have you ever heard negative things about somebody else? It may be tempting to listen to those tales and tell them to others. It's like a bite of chocolate; it can seem so tasty that you just want to enjoy it. That's how gossip works.

That's what this verse is warning us about. The words of one who gossips can seem tasty, but they "go down into the inmost body." If we've ever gossiped, then according to the Word of God, those words went down into our stomach. This lesson is not meant to step on anyone's toes, but we must know the truth. God's Word warns us of the danger of gossip — not just to the other person, but to us as well.

Proverbs 18:20 says, "A man's stomach shall be satisfied from the fruit of his mouth; from the produce of his lips he shall be filled." Take a moment to consider the words that come out of your mouth on any given day. Do you want the fruit of those words to be in your stomach? Do you want to taste and eat those words? The Bible says those words are going into your stomach.

Scientific studies have shown that when someone speaks words of thanksgiving, it has a positive effect on that person's blood pressure. Your words affect your mental health and your physical health too. So if words of thanksgiving have a positive effect on your body and mind, imagine what words of complaining and criticizing and gossip will do. These negative words have damaging effects on your well-being.

Study Your Words Before You Speak

These verses about gossip in Proverbs should not condemn us. Rather, God's Word is giving us instruction and warning. It's saying, "Don't gossip because you'll eat those toxic words, and those words are not healthy for you."

So what can we do to prevent ourselves from speaking "unhealthy" words? Proverbs 15:28 says, "The heart of the righteous studies how to answer, but the mouth of the wicked pours forth evil." When you received Jesus as your Lord and Savior, you became the righteousness of God in Christ (*see* 2 Corinthians 5:21). So when Proverbs 15:28 says "the heart of the righteous," it's talking about *you*. Maybe you don't do or say everything right — no one does. But because of your faith in the blood of Jesus, you have been made righteous. And the heart of the righteous "studies how to answer."

How are you going to stop yourself from gossiping? How can you stop yourself from criticizing your husband or correcting him or complaining? The Bible says you do this by *studying how to answer.* You must *teach and train your mouth.*

Studying takes time. You're going to have to consider your words first before you speak. You'll need to ask yourself: *What will happen if I say this? And if I say that instead, what will happen? Should I just keep my mouth closed right now? Do I acknowledge that my husband was right? Will there be more peace if I do that?*

Very often the things people argue about are not that important, and 15 minutes after they've argued, they've already forgotten what they were arguing about. So consider whether the thing you are arguing about — the thing you want to be *right* about — is going to matter in the long run. Remember the Bible says that as you argue and use your mouth to tear down other people, you cause trouble for your own soul. But you are righteous in Christ — you can study how to answer and avoid trouble.

Wise Words Are Sweet and Bring Well-Being

Proverbs 16:23 and 24 says, "The heart of the wise teaches his mouth, and adds learning to his lips. Pleasant words are like a honeycomb, sweetness to the soul and health to the bones." If you want to change how you are speaking to others and you're searching God's Word on the matter, then this passage is talking to you — and that makes you wise. And your kind words can be "like a honeycomb, sweetness to the soul and health to the bones" — health to *your* bones, *and* health to someone else's bones and sweetness to his or her soul. That's the power of the words you choose to speak — or refrain from speaking.

The Word of God is a lamp unto your feet; it's guiding your path (*see* Psalm 119:105). And it says that the words you speak are going down into your stomach and affecting your life. But you can train yourself to give wise answers and speak sweet words. You can study and learn how to answer with wisdom.

Here is a practical example of this Bible principle in action. Imagine you and another person, perhaps your husband, are about to get into an argument. The heat of the moment is rising quickly. Yet you can still *study* how to answer. You can say, "Could you excuse me for a minute? I'll be right back."

By excusing yourself for a moment, you are giving yourself space to *consider* your response. Maybe you need to step away for a few minutes and count to 10 (or even to 100). Maybe you can look in the mirror and ask yourself, "Is the point I'm trying to make really worth all this commotion — disrupting the peace in my family and home? Is it worth it to continue this argument?" You can smile at yourself, and say, "No, it's not." And then you can go back to that person calmly, and say, "You know what? I don't have anything else to say." There is no need to respond with something that will lead to an argument, because you've studied how to answer, and you have used wisdom to teach your lips.

A Soft Answer Silences Wrath

Reflecting again on Proverbs 31:26, it says, "She opens her mouth with wisdom, and on her tongue is *the law of kindness.*" There is a "law of kindness" that we can use when studying how to answer.

One such law is found in Proverbs 15:1 and 2, which says, "A soft answer turns away wrath, but a harsh word stirs up anger. The tongue of the wise uses knowledge rightly, but the mouth of fools pours forth foolishness." It's a biblical law that a soft answer turns away wrath.

In the example above concerning a heated situation, we see that one way to handle an argument is to take some time alone, and then return to the other person with a calm, gentle answer. A soft answer has so much power in it that it rebukes and silences wrath, but a harsh word stirs up anger. And all of this arises from such a small place on our body — our mouth.

These scriptures give us such great instruction for our life, and we can lean into what God's Word says. We don't have to be perfect; none of us has arrived. But we can lean our ear to His Word, and because we have done so, we can give a soft answer or walk away from arguments and establish peace in place of turmoil. Maybe we won't succeed every single time, but we can begin to practice this law.

The Word of God is truth and life, and we each can wisely choose to say, "I need to do something about *my* mouth and *my* feelings. I don't want to let *my* feelings control me. I want the Word of God to have the final say." And when we give the Word of God the last say, the soft answer He directs us to give has so much power that it can turn away wrath.

There are blessings to be found from the fruit that is produced from your obedience. Proverbs 12:14 says, "A man will be satisfied with good by the fruit of his mouth, and the recompense of a man's hands will be rendered to him." If your mouth brings goodness — such as praise, compliments, instruction, and kindness — then you'll be satisfied with the fruit of your mouth.

The Holy Spirit Will Teach You What To Say

More wisdom concerning our words can be found in Proverbs 12:18, which says, "There is one who speaks like the piercings of a sword, but the tongue of the wise promotes health." Have you ever spoken with somebody, and his or her negative words were like the piercing of a sword? Careless words can be so painful. But used with wisdom, your tongue has power, and it can promote health and bring healing to your body or the body of somebody else.

We started this lesson with Proverbs 18:21: "Death and life are in the power of the tongue, and those who love it will eat its fruit." Every day we get to choose what we want to receive — life or death. That's a lot of power for such a small member of the body. Our hands are bigger than our mouth, and so are our arms, our feet, our stomach, and so many other body parts. But which part of our body is the most powerful? The Bible says it's our tongue because it contains the power of life and death.

You may ask, "How can I tame my tongue and speak kindness to people who are unkind?" Remember, we are the righteousness of God in Christ Jesus, and we have the power of the Holy Spirit on the inside. We just read in Proverbs 15:28 and Proverbs 16:23 and 24 that the heart of the righteous teaches his mouth how to answer. If we yield to the Holy Spirit within us, He will teach us.

Take a moment and pray, *Holy Spirit, this person just said something to me that was so unkind. I want to retaliate and tell that person what I really think. But Holy Spirit, You live inside me, and I want to bring glory and honor to God, and I want to teach my mouth right now. I'm in training this very minute. Will You teach me what to say? Will You help me speak kindness to this person?* And He will do it!

Season Your Words With Grace

Ephesians 4:32 states, "And be kind to one another, tenderhearted, forgiving one another, even as God in Christ forgave you." The word "forgiving" here is a translation from the Greek word *charis*, which means *grace*. Another translation of this verse could be, "And be kind to one another, tenderhearted, *extending grace* to one another." We are to give grace to one another — grace in our actions and grace in our speech.

Inevitably, you will encounter someone who says something unkind to you, but you can give that person grace with your words. You can choose words that will extend grace to the other person — words of kindness, compassion, and mercy — not words laced with malice, criticism, or anger.

When you forgive someone, you are *gracing* him or her. Isn't that powerful? This verse means that when you are hit with unkind speech, you can say to yourself, "I am going to *respond*, but I'm not going to *react*. And I'm going to give *grace*." You can do that because of the power of the Holy Spirit who lives in you.

You can call on the Holy Spirit to give you power when you need it so you can give grace, His grace, to the other person. And when you open your mouth with wisdom, the law of kindness will be evident on your tongue. Praise the Lord!

STUDY QUESTIONS

> **Be diligent to present yourself approved to God, a worker who does not need to be ashamed, rightly dividing the word of truth.**
> **— 2 Timothy 2:15**

1. The importance of the tongue (and mouth and lips) is made evident throughout the Bible. Read the following scriptures and note the benefits or consequences of each verse. Write down the scriptures that most impact you.
   - 1 Peter 3:10
   - Ephesians 4:29
   - Proverbs 15:4
   - Proverbs 15:28
   - Proverbs 21:23

- Matthew 15:11
- Psalms 119:171,172
- Psalm 141:3

2. What is the common theme of the following scriptures: Proverbs 17:9; Proverbs 26:20; and Proverbs 18:8. Using the wisdom found in this lesson, how can this misuse of the tongue be avoided?
3. James 3:2-12 speaks in depth about taming your tongue. What stands out to you about this passage?

PRACTICAL APPLICATION

> But be doers of the word,
> and not hearers only, deceiving yourselves.
> —James 1:22

1. Follow David's example in Psalm 141:3 and cry out to God for help in the area of taming your tongue: "Set a guard, O Lord, over my mouth; keep watch over the door of my lips."
2. Proverbs 18:20 says, "A man's stomach shall be satisfied from the fruit of his mouth; from the produce of his lips he shall be filled." Reflect on the words that have come from your lips over the last 24 hours. Would you say the majority of those words promote life and health? Is your stomach satisfied? If not, what steps can you take today to fill your stomach with "good fruit"?
3. Take a moment to consecrate your mouth to Him by praying this prayer. *Father, I thank You so much for the power of Your Word. You have given me this Word and You have said in this Word that I can be delivered. You gave me the Holy Spirit, and He teaches and guides me into all truth. And right now I ask You, Holy Spirit, help me. Help me with my mouth. Help me put the law of kindness in my mouth and speak words of love, life, and kindness. In Jesus' name. Amen.*

LESSON 9

TOPIC
Help Me! My House Is a Mess — But Not for Long

SCRIPTURES

1. **Proverbs 31:27** — She watches over the ways of her household, and does not eat the bread of idleness.

2. **John 20:5-7** — And he, stooping down and looking in, saw the linen cloths lying there; yet he did not go in. Then Simon Peter came, following him, and went into the tomb; and he saw the linen cloths lying there, and the handkerchief that had been around His head, not lying with the linen cloths, but folded together in a place by itself.

3. **Proverbs 24:30-34** — I went by the field of the lazy man, and by the vineyard of the man devoid of understanding; and there it was, all overgrown with thorns; its surface was covered with nettles; its stone wall was broken down. When I saw it, I considered it well; I looked on it and received instruction: A little sleep, a little slumber, a little folding of the hands to rest; so shall your poverty come like a prowler, and your need like an armed man.

4. **Proverbs 26:13-16** — The lazy man says, "There is a lion in the road! A fierce lion is in the streets!" As a door turns on its hinges, so does the lazy man on his bed. The lazy man buries his hand in the bowl; it wearies him to bring it back to his mouth. The lazy man is wiser in his own eyes than seven men who can answer sensibly.

5. **Proverbs 21:25** — The desire of the lazy man kills him, for his hands refuse to labor.

6. **Proverbs 6:6-11** — Go to the ant, you sluggard! Consider her ways and be wise, which, having no captain, overseer or ruler, provides her supplies in the summer, and gathers her food in the harvest. How long will you slumber, O sluggard? When will you rise from your sleep? A little sleep, a little slumber, a little folding of the hands to sleep — so shall your poverty come on you like a prowler, and your need like an armed man.

SYNOPSIS

Proverbs 31:27 teaches that laziness is a trap that must be avoided if we are to accomplish the plan of God for our lives. As we look to God's Word, we see that it is filled with examples of the dangers of laziness, including poverty and lack, and how it can be avoided if one chooses to turn from it. Even Jesus took time to organize after being raised from the dead! His example and the wisdom found in Proverbs encourage us to avoid the lazy man's attitude and pursue the example of the ant — one of the hardest-working creatures on earth — so that we might be productive and blessed.

The emphasis of this lesson:

When we give in to laziness and make excuses for ourselves, we develop an unproductive habit that will eventually bring poverty to us. Thankfully, by obeying God's Word we can avoid the trap of laziness and pursue productive lives that benefit our household and others.

As we study Proverbs 31, we're reminded that God lifted Bathsheba to a place of being a teacher, not only to her son but to countless women throughout the centuries — including us! Although Bathsheba had committed adultery and was an accomplice to a murder, a liar, and deceived her nation, she truly repented. And the grace and forgiveness of God was so great on her and on King David that he became the greatest king of Israel and Bathsheba was able to give us this amazing teaching.

That is the grace of God, which we all can be so grateful for! When Jesus gave us His mercy, it wasn't because we deserved it — it was because we *didn't* deserve it. That's mercy. And we need to freely give mercy to one another in our relationships, especially in our homes. The Bible says if we give mercy, we will receive back mercy (*see* Matthew 5:7). Bathsheba received that mercy — and so can we.

A Tall Assignment

Consider Proverbs 31:27, which says, "She watches over the ways of her household, and does not eat the bread of idleness." This verse contains amazing instruction for us. The godly woman and wife watches over her household, and she is *not* lazy. Her thoughts are centered on how she can better her home. She asks herself questions, such as, "What is going on in my household?" "How can I help the people in my family?" "How can I run my home more smoothly?" and "How can I keep my house so that it is a place of peace and harmony where people *want* to be?"

Proverbs 31:27 does not contain many words, but it's a tall assignment. In her program, Denise spoke candidly from her personal insights on this topic by sharing her testimony:

> Many years ago when Rick and I got married, I was like most wives — I wanted to do everything perfectly. I was taking care of the house, learning to cook, and handling all the errands. But when I got pregnant with our first son, I had severe morning sickness, and I started making excuses for myself. I created bad habits. To be honest with you, I became a terrible housekeeper. I'm not proud to admit this, but my house did not have order to it. You would think that it would have changed after I had my son, or after having my second or third child, but it did *not* get better. The way we were living was not orderly.
>
> Right after we moved to the former Soviet Union, we visited the home of a sweet family. The family didn't have very much, but you could have eaten off the floor — it was so clean! They didn't have any paintings or trinkets to decorate their house, but they had stenciled the walls with beautiful patterns to make their house look pretty.
>
> I thought to myself, *I can't even say that I am bringing order to my own bedroom! There's no order for my children. I'm not teaching them to clean their room or to help clean the kitchen.* I saw the difference between my home and her home! But here's the thing: Before change can occur, you have to be able to see what the change can bring. And little by little, God was giving me a vision to help me *see*.
>
> I knew I was very disorderly. For example, if someone gave me flowers, I didn't even take the time to put them in a vase. I lacked the vision of how to keep a house — which meant I did *not* keep our house. And now we were living in another country, but I had met a woman who, although she and her family did not have many possessions, made her home look as perfect as possible. There was order in her home.
>
> I remember looking at the baseboards in her home and they were just perfect; they were painted and clean. Everything was orderly.

And I thought to myself, *That's what I want*. And at that moment, I was delivered of all that disorder, and *order came into my heart*.

When we got home from that trip, I spent 4 hours cleaning the kitchen. Then I spent 11 hours cleaning and organizing our bedroom, and then I spent 14 hours cleaning and organizing the boys' bedroom. I'm happy to say that my house has never, ever gone back to the disorderly mess it once was.

Please know, there is *no* condemnation or judgment for anyone who does not keep their house. There was a long season in my life that I didn't either. But I wanted order restored in my home, and *God delivered me* from the disorder.

Laziness Steals From Our Quality of Life

Do you struggle with laziness like I did? Do you find yourself unmotivated to get up and clean your kitchen or the rest of your house? Does laziness cause you to draw back from the responsibility of disciplining your children? Is it easier to make excuses than the phone call you know you need to make? If you're challenged in these areas, there is good news: You can face and conquer laziness.

Proverbs 31:27 makes it clear that this message is important for us to consider. When we begin to talk about laziness, our flesh doesn't like it. But we *have* to talk about it because if we give way to laziness it steals from our productivity and quality of life!

Consider John 20:5-7. Jesus had risen from the dead, and His disciples, Peter and John, went into the empty tomb. It says, "And he [John], stooping down and looking in, saw the linen cloths lying there; yet he did not go in. Then Simon Peter came, following him, and went into the tomb; and he saw the linen cloths lying there, and the handkerchief that had been around His head, not lying with the linen cloths, but folded together in a place by itself."

The headdress that was on Jesus for his burial was *folded* in an orderly manner. This means that after He arose from the dead, Jesus took the time to fold the headdress that had been on His head. You would think after Jesus rose from the dead that stopping to fold His burial linen would not be a high priority — but not for Jesus! Here, again, is an example of *order* in the Bible.

Instruction on Laziness From the Word of God

If even Jesus took time to keep things in order after being raised from the dead, then this principle must be very important. And it is! So if you're not taking care of some things you need to take care of and the delay is because of laziness, it's important to understand what the Bible says. And remember — there's no condemnation in Christ Jesus (*see* Romans 8:1). This lesson is not intended to judge you or condemn you but to help you enjoy a productive, fruitful life.

The Word of God offers valuable instruction about laziness and productivity, such as Proverbs 24:30-34. It says, "I went by the field of the lazy man, and by the vineyard of the man devoid of understanding; and there it was, all overgrown with thorns; its surface was covered with nettles; its stone wall was broken down. When I saw it, I considered it well; I looked on it and received instruction: A little sleep, a little slumber, a little folding of the hands to rest; so shall your poverty come like a prowler, and your need like an armed man."

This passage of Scripture was written by King Solomon, whom the Bible tells us was the wisest man in the world (*see* 1 Kings 4:29-31). In these verses, Solomon said that he had looked upon the house of the lazy man and saw how things were in disrepair. The fields and landscaping were overgrown; no one was taking care of the property. And then Soloman made a judgment about the result of laziness. He wrote, "So shall your poverty come like a prowler…" (Proverbs 24:34).

You Don't Want an Armed Man in Your Home

None of us wants a prowler to come into our home, look at our things, and say, "I'll take that, and I'll take that, and I'll take that." We don't want a thief in our house. But if we're lazy, the Bible says that poverty will come upon us like a thief to take from us.

We may make excuses to avoid the to-do list, and say, "I'm too tired. I need to take a nap." It's okay to take a nap once in a while — but not so many naps that our house falls into disorder or the simple things we should be taking care of are not being taken care of.

What happens when procrastination becomes a habit? Proverbs 24:34 says that your need will come on you "like an armed man." In other words, poverty will take you down. But, friend, you have the Spirit of God living in you! You were created to be an overcomer (*see* 1 John 5:4,5)! You're not supposed to be taken down — it's *you* who are supposed to take down the enemy and overcome the flesh that tries to steal from your life.

Don't Get Trapped in Your Own Excuses

Proverbs 26:13-16 informs us that "the lazy man says, 'There is a lion in the road! A fierce lion is in the streets!' As a door turns on its hinges, so does the lazy man on his bed. The lazy man buries his hand in the bowl; it wearies him to bring it back to his mouth. The lazy man is wiser in his own eyes than seven men who can answer sensibly." These verses explain the *attitude* of a lazy person, and it seems that a "lazy man" thinks quite highly of himself.

Do you know why a lazy man is conceited? It's because he has so much time to waste that he's caught up in his own thinking! He spends so much time daydreaming while whiling away the hours that he feels he's superior to those who are actually much smarter and more successful than he. He has time on his hands, and he uses that time to cast judgment on other people.

When we succumb to laziness, we become trapped in our own excuses. And as we saw in Proverbs 24:34, the result is that poverty comes on us like a prowler and takes us down, all the while considering ourselves to be smarter than those around us. It's not a pretty picture, is it?

Proverbs 26:14 says, "As a door turns on its hinges, so does the lazy man on his bed." To see this principle in action, just look at a door and watch how it hangs on its hinges. The hinges do all the work, while the door just swings one way and then the other. Just like that door, the lazy man rolls from one side of his bed to the other. As he sleeps, poverty comes, and bad habits are acquired that cause his home to be overgrown and underproductive. This is not God's will for us — not at all!

Go to the Ant

These scriptures make it clear that laziness is a thief. Yes, we have many responsibilities as daughters and sisters and wives and mothers. And as a result, it can feel easy to let our houses fall into disorder with dirty dishes in the sink or piles of unwashed laundry. Or perhaps we're not taking care of our children the way we should. Yet we cannot afford to make excuses, because if we do, laziness can become a *habit*. And if it becomes a habit, we become deceived by our own thinking. We believe that we're always right and smarter than those who are around us. Again, this is not God's will for our life.

Proverbs 21:25 tells us, "The desire of the lazy man kills him, for his hands refuse to labor." The lazy man *desires* to eat and drink and be clothed, but he *refuses* to work. He covets greedily all day long, but he lives and dies with his desires unsatisfied and envies those who have plenty through hard work and dedication. What is the response to a lazy man's attitude? According to Proverbs 6, it is to "go to the ant."

Why would the Bible tell us to go to the ant? Proverbs 6:6-11 says, "Go to the ant, you sluggard! Consider her ways and be wise, which, having no captain, overseer or ruler, provides her supplies in the summer, and gathers her food in the harvest. How long will you slumber, O sluggard? When will you rise from your sleep? A little sleep, a little slumber, a little folding of the hands to sleep — so shall your poverty come on you like a prowler, and your need like an armed man." Notice the last verse repeats the same warning found in Proverbs 24:34: "So shall your poverty come like a prowler, and your need like an armed man." Soloman must have thought this wisdom was important enough to mention twice!

Let's return to the subject of the ant. Ants are the most hard-working insects in existence, and they have keen oversight and foresight for the other ants in their colony. They work quietly without showiness, and they work unweariedly until their work is done. Have you ever watched ants before? They're capable of carrying something that is ten times their size. In other words, ants are not lazy! And neither should we be lazy. So let's use the ant as our example; let's work hard for our family and be diligent about the tasks we have before us. And God will bless and establish the work of our hands (*see* Psalm 90:17).

STUDY QUESTIONS

**Be diligent to present yourself approved to God, a worker who does not need to be ashamed, rightly dividing the word of truth.
— 2 Timothy 2:15**

1. Read Proverbs 10:4; Proverbs 18:9; Proverbs 20:4; Proverbs 20:13; Proverbs 21:27; and Proverbs 15:19. Note the words used to describe

the fruit of a "diligent" person and the words used to describe the fruit of a "lazy" person.
2. Proverbs 12:24 says, "The hand of the diligent [industrious, hard-working, earnest] will rule, but the lazy [idle, sluggish, lethargic] man will be put to forced labor." Give an example of someone in the Bible who would be considered "diligent." Can you think of an example in the Bible of someone who would be considered "lazy"?

PRACTICAL APPLICATION

**But be doers of the word,
and not hearers only, deceiving yourselves.
— James 1:22**

1. Read Proverbs 24:30-34. Is there an area in your life you would consider to be "overgrown" or "covered with nettles"? What steps can you take to "clear away the brush" and "reseed" for a healthier harvest?
2. In this lesson, Denise highlighted the diligence of ants and their positive example. She shared vital instruction from the Word of God that laziness is dangerous and can open the door to a thief called poverty. If you've struggled with laziness (or its cousin, procrastination) in any area of your life, ask the Lord for forgiveness and help to change that unfruitful behavior. Pray: *Father God, I've been lazy in the area of _____. Please forgive me. I've created excuses for the lack and disorder in my life, but I want to be productive and diligent and restore order to every area of my life. I turn from laziness and choose diligence, and I know this is possible through You and with Your strength. Lord, I give You the praise for the work that You are doing and will continue to do in my life. In Jesus' name. Amen.*

LESSON 10

TOPIC
Practical Wisdom To Build Up Your House

SCRIPTURES

1. **Psalm 103:12** — As far as the east is from the west, so far has He removed our transgressions from us.
2. **Proverbs 31:11,12** — The heart of her husband safely trusts her; so he will have no lack of gain. She does him good and not evil all the days of her life.
3. **Matthew 7:1-5** — "Judge not, that you be not judged. For with what judgment you judge, you will be judged; and with the measure you use, it will be measured back to you. And why do you look at the speck in your brother's eye, but do not consider the plank in your own eye? Or how can you say to your brother, 'Let me remove the speck from your eye'; and look, a plank is in your own eye? Hypocrite! First remove the plank from your own eye, and then you will see clearly to remove the speck from your brother's eye."
4. **Proverbs 31:16** — She considers a field and buys it; from her profits she plants a vineyard.

SYNOPSIS

The wisdom found in Proverbs 31 allows us to appreciate the transforming power of God's forgiveness to help us start afresh and be renewed in our roles as godly women, wives, and mothers. And we can apply this practical wisdom every day in our relationships and marriage — wisdom such as staying committed to working things out, considering our words and actions, evaluating ourselves rather than judging others, or creating a safe place where our husband can hear from God — so we can experience His peace and blessings in our homes.

The emphasis of this lesson:

We can lean on God's power and His wisdom to guide us in practical ways as we love our husband, seek peace, and cultivate the wise actions and words of a truly blessed, godly, virtuous woman and wife.

As Far as the East Is From the West

Bathsheba wasn't a perfect woman — quite the opposite! We know she was an adulteress, an accomplice to a murder, a liar, and a deceiver to a whole nation. But what a revelation it is to observe the power of forgiveness that transformed Bathsheba.

In Second Samuel 11 and 12, we read about David's devious behavior as he planned to have Uriah, Bathsheba's husband, killed. Bathsheba was probably an accomplice to that murder because she and David needed to cover their sin. Their story reveals how ugly human nature can be. But what happened to David and Bathsheba? They repented. And what does repentance do? *It removes the mark of sin on our life.*

In Psalm 103, we see the amazing heart of God concerning forgiveness. Verse 12 reads, "As far as the east is from the west, so far has He removed our transgressions from us." What a fantastic image of God's forgiveness! The east and west will never, ever meet! And when we approach God with a repentant heart, He removes our transgressions from us. Those sins are never going to meet up with us again.

A repentant heart is what enabled Bathsheba to be lifted to the level of teacher and well-qualified to instruct her son on how to be a compassionate and kind king, how to maintain his strength, and how he should not be overtaken by strong drink. If she had been under the burden of her past sin, how could she have the confidence to teach her son those things? And for thousands of years, women have looked to this chapter and prayed over these scriptures to learn how they might become virtuous women.

We Have Been Forgiven Much

Proverbs 31 is full of godly wisdom which came from an imperfect woman — one who'd been forgiven much. What a beautiful picture of the power of the forgiveness of God! In her program, Denise shared a story of repentance, God's forgiveness, and the unwavering truth of God's Word.

I heard about a person who committed adultery against their spouse. This person did break the marriage covenant, but this person also repented. An unwise friend came along and said, "I know that you've repented, but don't get your expectations too high. I just want you to know that your life is never going to be the same. It's like you're always going to be limping in your soul somewhere."

That's a lie from the devil. The blood of Jesus is more powerful than any sin! His Blood cleanses us from *all* sin, *all* unrighteousness (*see* 1 John 1:7,9) and does not leave us limping!

When we came to Jesus, repented before Him, and believed on Him, He said, in essence, "I have removed your sin from you as far as the east is from the west. In My eyes, you are righteous!" That doesn't mean we should take the liberty to go and sin. *No!* Don't go and sin! Romans 6:15 says, "What then? Shall we sin, because we are not under the law, but under grace? *God forbid.*"

But God has set us in a place of righteousness (*see* 2 Corinthians 5:21). And in that place of righteousness, you can say, "God, I'm sorry. I messed up. I sinned against You. I repent," because the blood of Jesus has washed you clean (*see* 1 John 1:7-9). Denise explained, "That person who told my friend they would never be the same and would always have some kind of scar on their soul was wrong!" That kind of thinking is *not* the truth because of the *power of the blood of Jesus.*

And that's what Bathsheba experienced — an amazing deliverance and forgiveness of *all* that she had done. That forgiveness raised her to a place of confidence where she could share what she had learned, and thousands of years later we're still receiving from her teaching. How magnificent that is!

Close the Back Door With Your Commitment

Proverbs 31:11 and 12 says, "The heart of her husband safely trusts her; so he will have no lack of gain. She does him good and not evil all the days of her life." How is that possible? It's because this virtuous woman made a commitment. Denise shared in her program:

> When my husband Rick and I got married, we made a covenant with one another. We made a commitment before God and to one another that we would never speak about divorce. By doing

so, we closed the back door to divorce. Has our marriage been perfect? No. Have we had times when there were things we had to work through and make better? Yes. But during those times, the back door was always closed. There was never an option to escape.

You are counted as a wise woman for studying Proverbs 31 and working through these lessons on marriage and godly womanhood. You are operating in wisdom when you declare, "I've made a commitment to my marriage. I've made a covenant with my husband. And no, things aren't perfect, but I close the back door to this marriage. I don't intend to walk away."

What does that commitment do to the heart of a wife or the heart of the husband? It tells us we'll have to work through some things, but it inspires us to come to God and seek His help. It encourages us to pray, "God, I may not understand what's going on in my marriage, but I've closed the back door. I'm not escaping from this marriage, so God, talk to me." By doing so, we close that back door, but we open the door of our own heart to seek after God for His answers. Now *that's* a commitment.

Make Your Heart a Place of Safety for Your Husband

Notice again that Proverbs 31:11 says, "The heart of her husband safely trusts her...." Imagine a warm fireplace in a home. The husband comes in on a cold day, and there's a fire in the fireplace waiting for him, which brings him warmth and comfort. Instead of wanting to run away from his home, this husband wants to run *to* his home because it's a safe place for him. Like this fireplace, a virtuous wife is the heart of the home and provides a safe and secure place that her husband can run to. His heart can safely trust in his wife.

Wives, how will the heart of your husband safely trust you? It happens as you *accept him as he is.* Now that does *not* mean you should accept a pornography addiction or the physical or sexual abuse of your children or yourself. No! Do *not* accept that! *In such situations, you need to seek help.*

No, I'm not talking about accepting abuse, but there may be situations where your husband needs to grow — as we all do. Perhaps he drinks a little too much or he curses. Maybe you don't like how he eats, or he's gained too much weight. Maybe he doesn't read the Bible or go to church, or he may not like your mother. There are many things other people do that tempt us to say, "I don't like that, and I can't accept that. You need to be more like me." That is called a judgmental attitude. And what does a judgmental attitude do to a marriage? It builds walls.

Judge Yourself, Not Others

Do you know what Jesus says about judgment? His words on this topic in Matthew 7:1-5 are very straightforward and instructive. Jesus says, "Judge not, that you be not judged. For with what judgment you judge, you will be judged; and with the measure you use, it will be measured back to you. And why do you look at the speck in your brother's eye, but do not consider the plank in your own eye? Or how can you say to your brother, 'Let me remove the speck from your eye'; and look, a plank is in your own eye? Hypocrite! First remove the plank from your own eye, and then you will see clearly to remove the speck from your brother's eye."

Denise shared that she studied this passage of scripture many times because she could see in herself a tendency to want to judge. At one point or another, we may *all* find ourselves tempted to judge someone. Perhaps we want to judge our spouse or somebody else. But we don't have the right to judge others because, according to Matthew 7:1-5, we have a plank in our own eye.

If you have a board in front of your eyes, how would you even see the speck that's in someone else's eye? You *can't* see the speck in that person's eye! Why? Because of the plank in your *own* eye! If you're so focused on the speck — a flaw — in the other person, you'll fail to realize there's a plank — the *many* flaws — in you!

When it comes to judging others, Jesus said, "How can you judge others? You can't see clearly!" No, we can't see clearly, but we deceive ourselves and think, *Oh yes, I see so clearly that you are wrong. I see it. I'm thinking about it. And now, I'm going to talk to you about it.*

Let's look again at what Jesus said in Matthew 7:4. He said, "Or how can you say to your brother, 'Let me remove the speck from your eye'; and look, a plank is in your own eye?" So not only do we think we have the right to *tell* someone else what we think is wrong with him or her, but we're brazen enough to *show* this person how to change it. We're going to step into this person's business to "help" him or her change.

We might think, *Well, I'm supposed to help them change it. What they're doing is not right, and I need to teach them, and I need to correct them.* But notice that Jesus said, in essence, "How can you help them change the speck you see in their eye when there's a board in your own eye?" The Bible has a name for someone who behaves like this — a hypocrite. God says we're *hypocrites* if we are trying to correct others without first correcting ourselves.

Make Room for God To Speak

In her program, Denise offered encouragement about being willing to judge ourselves instead of others, and we can follow her example. She said, "When I see these scriptures, I start thinking about what Jesus did for me and what wrong I've done. I see His mercy and grace. And I say, 'Lord, You've done so much for me! How can I look at someone else's fault and be judgmental toward this person? God, forgive me.' And usually what happens is that I get so busy correcting and changing my own flaws that I'm no longer focused on the flaw in the other person." In other words, if we put our face in the mirror of God's Word, it makes it difficult to see the flaws of others.

What does it do for a marriage when the wife judges herself instead of her spouse? It helps a woman who has been griping and complaining to close her mouth. And because her husband is not preoccupied with hearing her, *it allows him to hear God.*

Wives, if you allow some silence now and then by closing your mouth, it will make room for your husband to hear from God. That's one way you can do him good and not evil all the days of your life (*see* Proverbs 31:12). It's hard to hear God's voice when another person is always speaking; he may just need a little peace and quiet. If you constantly fill your time together by speaking to your husband, you could hinder him from hearing from God because God speaks in "a still, small voice" (1 Kings 19:12).

Consider Your Words

Again, Proverbs 31:16 says, "She considers a field and buys it; from her profits she plants a vineyard." You may never have purchased a field or even planted a garden, but you *can* consider your actions. You have that opportunity every single minute of every single day.

In a previous lesson, Denise gave the example of having a conversation with your friends, and your husband begins to tell a story. You think to yourself, *That's not how the story went. I want to clarify the facts, so I need to correct my husband.* But when you correct your husband in public, he becomes offended. Maybe you argue all the way home. You could have had a romantic evening together, but now you're not even speaking because you offended him and embarrassed him in front of people.

What if we consider what it is we're going to say *before* we speak? That's what this verse in Proverbs is saying — the wise, virtuous woman *considers*. She *thinks* about what she's going to do before she does it. She *contemplates* what she's going to say before she says it.

In that same scenario, imagine that a wife hears her husband telling a story, and she remembers it differently. She *wants* to say, "No, it didn't happen like that, sweetheart. It happened like this." But she *considers* her words first. And she thinks, *Is this story really that important? Are those facts going to even matter in 20 minutes? Are they going to matter in two hours? Are they going to matter in two years? Probably not. I could close my mouth and maintain the peace. I can enjoy this evening with our friends and my husband, and maybe have a wonderful time with my husband when we get home tonight.*

That is a Proverbs 31 woman in action. She considers what it is that's coming out of her mouth, and she considers her actions. The Bible says the mouth is so powerful that death and life come out of it. And we can choose death, or we can choose life. Think about the wisdom found in Proverbs 31, and let it guide you as you grow as a godly, virtuous woman who is well able to be a blessing to your husband and your household.

STUDY QUESTIONS

> **Be diligent to present yourself approved to God, a worker who does not need to be ashamed, rightly dividing the word of truth.**
> **— 2 Timothy 2:15**

1. Review the four scriptures in the Scripture section of this lesson (Psalm 103:12; Proverbs 31:11,12; Matthew 7:1-5; and Proverbs 31:16). Taking into account what you've learned in this lesson, how would you explain (or expound upon) each scripture to someone who did not understand them?

2. "The wise woman builds her house, but the foolish pulls it down with her hands" (Proverbs 14:1). In what ways does a wise woman build her home? In what ways does a foolish woman tear down her home?
3. What does Romans 2:1 tell us about judging others?

PRACTICAL APPLICATION

> But be doers of the word,
> and not hearers only, deceiving yourselves.
> —James 1:22

1. If you're in the habit of being quick to judge or criticize, consider the possibilities if you exchanged that habit for choosing to shine the mirror of God's Word on yourself before speaking. What might this do for your relationships? Your marriage? Your husband? What might this do for *you*?
2. Read the intimate conversation between the Lord and Elijah in First Kings 19:9-12. Elijah needed direction, and he found it in God's "still small voice." What is one way you can respect or make room for your husband's quiet time with God to give him the space he needs to receive direction from Him?
3. Of the ten lessons in this study guide, which lesson impacted you the most? Review that lesson and ask God to continue to bring change in your life as you meditate on the scriptures and practical wisdom Denise imparted in that lesson. Share what you've learned with a friend or with your husband and allow it to bless that person as well!

***If you or your children are experiencing physical, sexual, or emotional abuse, please seek help. You need to protect yourself and your children from harm. Contact a counselor, pastor, or domestic-violence hotline and ask for help.

CLAIM YOUR FREE RESOURCE!

As a way of introducing you further to the teaching ministry of Rick Renner, we would like to send you FREE of charge his teaching, "How To Receive a Miraculous Touch From God" on CD or as an MP3 download.

In His earthly ministry, Jesus commonly healed *all* who were sick of *all* their diseases. In this profound message, learn about the manifold dimensions of Christ's wisdom, goodness, power, and love toward all humanity who came to Him in faith with their needs.

☑ YES, I want to receive Rick Renner's monthly teaching letter!

Simply scan the QR code to claim this resource or go to:
renner.org/claim-your-free-offer

WITH US!

renner.org

facebook.com/rickrenner • facebook.com/rennerdenise
youtube.com/rennerministries • youtube.com/deniserenner
instagram.com/rickrrenner • instagram.com/rennerministries_
instagram.com/rennerdenise

www.ingramcontent.com/pod-product-compliance
Lightning Source LLC
Chambersburg PA
CBHW071627040426
42452CB00009B/1517